ME

ME

Katrin Behrend

Guinea Pigs

How to Care for Them,
Feed Them, and
Understand Them

Photographs: Karin Skogstad
Illustrations: Renate Holzner

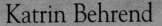

CONTENTS

1

**What you Need to
Know Before
Acquiring a Guinea Pig**

The Guinea Pig's Origin   8
The Pet of the Incas   8
How the "Indian Pig"
   Came to Europe   9
One Animal, Many Names   10
Zoological Classification   12
Wild Relatives   12

**Things to Think About
   Before Buying a
   Guinea Pig**   14
Helpful Tips   14
Are Two Guinea Pigs
   Happier Than One?   14
Male or Female?   16
If You Have Other Pets   19

Guinea Pigs and Children   20
Vacation Care   20

**The Law and the Pet
   Owner**   24

**Where to Get a
   Guinea Pig?**   26
Domestic or Purebred
   Guinea Pig?   26
Where to Find the Kind
   of Guinea Pig You Want   26
Let the Buyer Beware   28

Good Health Is Important   30

Profile of the Guinea Pig   32
Characteristics of Purebred
   Guinea Pigs   32
What Is a Breed Standard   32
Breeds   32

2

**Proper Care
and Grooming**

Equipment and Housing   44
The Cage: A Happy
   Home   44
Indoor Exercise   52
Summer Vacation on the
   Balcony   53
Outdoor Enclosure (Pen)   54

**The Well-Groomed
   Guinea Pig**   56

Good Nutrition   64

**Preventive Care and
   Health Problems**   70
The Right Diet for
   Good Health   70
Health Problems for
   Humans   70
The First Symptoms of
   Illness   72

The Sick Guinea Pig   76

**Planned Breeding of
   Guinea Pigs**   78
Breeding Purebred
   Guinea Pigs   78
Life as a Couple   81
Pregnancy   83

Birth   84
How Often May the
    Female Be Bred?   85
Development of the Young   86

3 Understanding Your Pet and Keeping It Busy

Becoming Familiar with Behavioral Problems   90
Anatomical Characteristics   90
Adapted for Survival   91
Fighting Over Rank Order   91
Survival Strategies   93
Guinea Pig Language   93
Body Language   96

Getting the Guinea Pig Settled Properly   98
The New Home   98
Guinea Pigs and Children   98
Hand-taming Your Pet   100
Becoming Acquainted
    with Other Guinea Pigs   101

Training a Guinea Pig   104

Great Ideas for Playing with Your Guinea Pig   108

The Right Way to Solve Behavioral Problems   112

Of General Importance

My Guinea Pig   118
Index   120
Useful Addresses and
    Information   125
Important Note   127
Publishing Information   127

Children's Corner

Will a Guinea Pig
    Become Tame?   23
How Do Offspring
    Get Here?   28
Why Do Guinea Pigs
    Like to Go into
    Caves?   51
Why Do Guinea Pigs
    Chatter with Their
    Teeth?   55
Are Guinea Pigs Clever
    Animals?   63
What Are Nidifugous
    Animals?   86
Can Guinea Pigs Get
    Nasty?   93
Can Guinea Pigs Be
    Trained?   103

What You Need

to Know Before Acquiring a Guinea Pig

The guinea pig came originally from South America. The following chapter will tell you everything else you need to know about this popular pet.

Guinea pigs are most at home when they have company

The Guinea Pig's Origins

Guinea pigs and humans became friends around 10,000 years ago. And these good-natured, sociable animals continue to be great favorites of pet owners today.

The Pet of the Incas

Originally, guinea pigs came from Central and South America. Their ancestors, the wild cavies, are common throughout that geographical area. In fact, their natural habitat extends from the Atlantic coast of Uruguay and Argentina, through the dry pampas in the interior of the continent, to the rocky Andean regions in the west and north, where caves abound. Without a doubt, these animals, which are members of the enormous family of rodents, established themselves on Earth 35 to 40 million years ago. However, it is only recently that we were able to determine when the transition from wild cavy to domestic guinea pig took place. The

Although the large Mara looks very different from the guinea pig, it is actually related to the domestic guinea pig.

The weasel guinea pig (*Galea musteloides*), native to Argentina, is also a close relative of the domestic guinea pig.

transition from wild cavy to domestic pig only took place between 9,000 and 3,000 B.C., as archaeological digs have disclosed. That sounds like a very long time, but an animal as shy as the wild cavy doesn't turn into a house pet overnight (see Survival Strategy, page 93).

More than anything else, it was probably scraps of food that drew the wild cavies to humans in Peru more than 10,000 years ago, before the Inca period. During excavations, archaeologists discovered pens that even offered these animals a space with protection against the sun in which to exercise, though they were not yet domesticated.

Little by little, people proceeded to breed guinea pigs and to put them to use. Among the Quechua, the original ruling class of the Incan Empire, they were viewed not only as an item that lent variety to the bill of fare, but also as sacrificial animals.

How the "Indian Pig" Came to Europe

Tame guinea pigs did not remain a specialty of the Incas alone. The Indians of Panama also kept them as pets. The accounts of the Spanish conquerors, who crossed southern Central America in search of treasure, also mention small, squealing animals that they encountered in houses everywhere. Probably the *conquistadores* did not intend to bring these creatures back to Spain along with gold, silver, and jewels. Nonetheless, a few guinea pigs must have arrived in Europe as early as 1540, because Swiss zoologist Konrad Gesner wrote *On the Indian Rabbit or Piglet* in 1554. People assumed that Columbus had discovered India on his sea route; therefore, everything that came from there was "Indian."

9

We don't know whether descendants of those first "immigrants" still survive. However, records show that guinea pigs came to Holland about 1670, from what was, in those days, Dutch Guyana. Thinking that these cute, friendly creatures would make superb playmates for their children, Dutch merchants took them back to the Netherlands.

Soon people began to breed them because a great deal of money could be made selling them to buyers in France and England. At first, only the rich could afford to buy them. But since the guinea pigs reproduced so rapidly, dealing in them soon became financially unattractive. As they spread across Europe, the popularity of the little creatures also grew—not least of all because they were so extremely easy to keep, house, feed, and breed.

One Animal, Many Names

In almost every case, the name people assigned this little creature in each country is misleading and is completely unrelated to the animal's true nature.

The capybara or carpincho (genus *Hydrochoerus*) is the largest of all rodents. It lives in Eastern Panama and South America, east of the Andes. This "water hog," as it is sometimes called, is related to the guinea pig.

The Domestic Guinea Pig (*Cavia aperea porcellus*): A Profile

Order:	Rodents (Rodentia)
Suborder:	Cavy rodents (Caviomorpha)
Family:	Cavies (Caviidae)
Subfamily:	True cavies (Caviinae)
Genus:	*Cavia*
Species:	*Cavia* aperea
Length:	8.66 to 13.78 inches (22–35 cm)
Weight:	Male up to 63.5 ounces (1800 g); female up to 38.8 ounces (1100 g)
Gestation:	About 68 days
Young:	From one to more than seven per birth
Birth weight:	1.4 to 3.5 ounces (40–100 g)
Characteristics:	Various colors and patterns; hair textures, and lengths
Diet:	Grasses, hay, leaves, bark, fruits, roots, blossoms, seeds
Life-style:	Pack animal
Life expectancy:	Five to 10 years
Distribution:	South America and Central America
Domestication:	Between 9000 and 3000 B.C.

Today the term cavy is used more and more. Derived from the guinea pig's scientific name, it comes closest to the truth. "Cavy"—derived from the Latin *cavus* = cave—refers to guinea pigs, members of the family Caviidae, as cave dwellers (see the Zoological Classification, page 12).

The following explanations are a summary of all the attempts at interpretation that have accumulated over time.

In German-speaking areas the name *Meerschweinchen* denotes a small animal that has rounded contours. Like a little pig (*Schweinchen*), it has a sagging belly, short legs, and squeals. *Meer* (sea, ocean) may refer to the animal's place of origin on the other side of the Atlantic Ocean. However, it may also be a distortion of *Möhren* (carrots).

In Holland it was first called *Meerzwijn*, then *Guinees biggetje* because the piglet was once sold at the high price of one guinea, an English gold coin no longer in circulation. Today the term currently used is Cavia, the Latin name of the genus.

According to another story, guinea was a confusion of the animal's country of origin—

11

Dutch Guyana—with Guinea, the colony in Africa. The flip side of the golden coin is the sad fact that the English "guinea pig," like the German word "Versuchskaninchen," refers to a lab animal, a subject for experimentation.

The French call the guinea pig *cochon d'Inde*, "pig of India."

The Spanish use the word *conejillo de Indias*, "little rabbit of India," which is closest to this animal's zoological classification as a member of the rodent family but still expresses the erroneous belief that Columbus had found the western part of India.

Zoological Classification

The guinea pig belongs to the rodent family. Common to all rodents is a set of teeth with rootless front incisors that constantly regrow and are separated from the molars by a large space (diastema).

Within the order of rodents, we are chiefly interested here in the wild cavies of the genus *Cavia*. The most common species is *Cavia aperea*, found both in flat country and in mountainous regions. One subspecies is the Tschudi cavy (*Cavia aperea tschudii*), native to south central Chile.

The Tschudi cavy appears at altitudes of up to almost 14,000 feet (4200 m), has a slender body and great agility in climbing and leaping, and lives in small groups of 5 to 10 animals, in burrows in the earth, which they dig themselves or take over from other animals. They live on grasses, herbs, and other vegetation.

Wild Relatives

While it would be impossible to list all the relatives of the domestic guinea pig in this book, I would like to introduce a few of them, because they look and act so different than you would expect.

Rock cavy: Also known as *Kerodon rupestris*, it inhabits

Guinea pigs have the "harelip" typical of all rodents.

The southern dwarf guinea pig (*Microcavia australis*) is only half the size of our tame little squealer (guinea pig).

negotiate completely smooth cement and glass brick walls 4 feet (1.20 m) high."

Mara: Also known as the Patagonian cavy, at first glance it resembles a hare. It can reach a length of up to 29 inches (75 cm) and a weight of 20–35 pounds (9–16 kg). It lives in dry grasslands and brushlands, where it digs deep, wide burrows for itself. It can run fast and jump as far as 6.6 feet (2 m).

Capybara: As the largest living rodent, it can grow to 4 feet (1.3 m) long and weigh 110 pounds (50 kg). The Tupi word *capybara*, means "master of the grasses." Water, however, is its element. It is an excellent swimmer and diver.

Tree porcupines: These arboreal, or tree-inhabiting, animals, are native to Central and South America. In some species, the hairs on the body and tail have been transformed into spines, often barbed, that are an effective weapon against most enemies. Some species have a tail with which they can grip tree branches tightly.

dry, rocky hills and stays hidden under boulders or in rock clefts. Sure-footed rock cavies can leap from rock to rock and climb into low trees to eat leaves. Ludwig Heck, director of the Berlin Zoo, describes their skill in climbing in *Brehms Tierleben:* "By means of several successive crosswise leaps, these little rascals easily

Things to Think About Before Buying a Guinea Pig

Unfortunately, guinea pigs cannot choose their owners. A pet guinea pig is dependent on the care and affection of humans.

Helpful Tips

You need to ask yourself whether you can meet all the prerequisites for providing a guinea pig with good, appropriate care. The following ten points can help you make the right decision.

1 A guinea pig can live as long as 8–10 years. Are you ready for commitment?

2 A guinea pig needs a cage, which can be expensive.

3 The cage must be kept clean at all times, and the food must always be fresh. This means time and effort on your part.

4 A guinea pig needs someone to "talk" to and something to do, so that it does not lead a dull life.

5 When you let the guinea pig out in your home to exercise, it may chew on your furniture and wallpaper, shed on your carpet, and leave behind little puddles or sack pellets. Can you be tolerant?

6 If you give the guinea pig to your child, you should feel jointly responsible for it.

7 Keep in mind that someone will have to take care of your guinea pig while you are on vacation.

8 If the guinea pig gets sick, you have to take it to the veterinarian. Treatment may be expensive.

9 If you already have other pets, they might not get along with a guinea pig.

10 Before acquiring a guinea pig, make sure that neither you nor any other member of your family is allergic to it (see page 70).

Are Two Guinea Pigs Happier Than One?

Guinea pigs are sociable creatures, and in their natural habitat they live together in clans. In general, they get along very well together; they like to cuddle up or to chase each other around, squealing and making cooing or purring sounds.

Consequently, it is inappropriate to keep a member of this species in a cage by itself. If it is alone, you must spend a great deal of time with it.

■ A single guinea pig is more suitable for a child that wants a playmate. It will become tame more quickly, and the trust that develops between it and

Our guinea pig looks charming and perky. It's not surprising that it captures everyone's heart.

the child will be lasting (see Guinea Pigs and Children, page 20).

If it turns out that too little time is left for the animal because of homework or other demands on time, you should consider acquiring a second guinea pig.

■ A guinea pig couple will produced offspring four or five times a year. Young guinea pigs are charming, but where will you put them? It is absolutely essential to get rid of them before puberty; otherwise, they will reproduce on a vast scale (see page 86). That makes sense only if you are planning to breed guinea pigs. Alternatively, you can have one of the animals spayed or neutered (see page 18).

■ Two females will get along quite well.

■ Two males also can be kept together in one cage—provided they are from the same litter or were placed together while still young. If they have had no contact with females during or since puberty, they will get along well as adults. This rule also holds true if you want to give an old male a young one as a companion. The two will get along fine until one of them—even for a

brief time—has been near a female. Then they are likely to come to blows (see page 91). If a guinea pig is neutered after puberty, it will still fight with other old males.

Male or Female?

There are a few points that you need to consider in making your decision.

A male, or boar, is generally larger, heavier, and livelier than a female. Sometimes a bit more patience is needed to gain his trust. When he reaches puberty, the boar gives off a strong odor. Neutering the animal will reduce this odor (see page 18).

Of all the guinea pigs only the wild guinea pig (*Cavia aperea tschudii*) has become a house pet.

Photograph on the right: The Incas bred brown- and white-spotted guinea pigs and sacrificied them to the sun god.

Differences Between Wild Cavies and Domestic Guinea Pigs

	Wild Cavy	Domestic Guinea Pig
Body	Slender, with longer hind legs	Rounded, plumper overall, thicker legs, and larger feet
Head	Sharp-nosed	More rounded, with bigger ears
Coat	Short-haired, rough, dark gray-brown to black ("wild" color)	Short- or long-haired, smooth or with whorls, many colors
Eye color	Dark	Dark or red
Internal organs	Small stomach, short small intestine, long cecum and large intestine	Large stomach, long small intestine, short cecum and large intestine
Feces	Plentiful	Scant
Gestation	60 days	68 days
Birth weight	1.4 to 1.8 ounces (40–50 g)	2.9 to 3.2 ounces (85–90 g)
Special feature	Able to jump to a height of about 30 inches (¾ m)	

A female, or sow, will stay smaller, and upon entering puberty her odor will be less pungent than the male's. Many people say that the female is more affectionate, but there is no proof of this. Both the personality of the individual animal and the amount of attention you devote to your pet play a part. In addition, it's not uncommon to hear of people buying a female that is already pregnant. Another version of this story is that children get together to play with their guinea pigs; if one of the pets is a male, it may mate with the female. If a child does this on purpose, don't scold him; just explain exactly what the consequences could be.

Some Comments on Spaying and Neutering

Castration—removal of the testicles or ovaries—is advisable if you own a pair of guinea pigs but are unwilling to deal

with their offspring constantly. Keep the following in mind:

■ Spaying a female is a difficult, high-risk procedure. As a rule, a veterinarian will advise against such an operation.

■ Generally, a healthy male will be unaffected by the surgery. But any pre-existing, undetected disease is certain to manifest itself afterward.

To affect the odor, neutering should be performed by the eighth month of life.

Caution: A boar can mate for up to six weeks after the operation. He will continue to court a sow, but after castration his disposition will be more placid, and his smell will be less acrid. In general, he will get along better with other males; though biting is not out of the question. In some instances, the boar may become lazy and fat. Boars that are castrated before the age of three months will not grow as large as non-neutered males.

Sows are equally compatible with unneutered and neutered males, since the latter do not give up their courting behavior. Sometimes, however, a sow will dominate a neutered boar, taking food from him.

Fruit is healthy and also tastes good when it's dinner for two, because guinea pigs rarely fight about food.

TIP

It's not all that easy to determine the sex of a young guinea pig. Near the anal area, carefully press the stomach with your index finger. If the penis appears, it's a male. In the female, the sex organ is a rather long Y-shaped slit that extends to the anal opening.

Sexing Guinea Pigs

Because adult animals differ in size, you can make your gender selection on the basis of outward appearance. Young animals are all the same size.

A breeder or an experienced pet store dealer can help determine the sex of your pet. But if you are given a guinea pig by friends or neighbors, you need to know how to sex the animal yourself.

If You Have Other Pets

Close friendships can develop with some animals; with others, caution is in order.

Dwarf rabbit: In general, guinea pigs get along well with them. The rabbit will protect its little friend, nestle with it, and lick it clean. However, it is not uncommon for the rabbit to bite its cagemate.

Dog: If you already have a dog, you'll have to help him get used to the new housemate. If both animals are still young, that usually can be done. But if your dog is already established in your home, you should avoid giving it any cause for jealousy. Guard dogs are said to get along especially well with guinea pigs, but don't count on that. Guinea pigs running around can arouse the dog's hunting instinct—and a single bite is enough to kill the little creature.

Cat: Depending on its size, a cat will first approach the guinea pig as prey, swiping at it with its paw, possibly injuring it seriously. If the two grow up together, they usually will get along well. Guinea pigs that are kept outdoors must always be protected from cats.

Mice and rats: It is possible to keep them in the same cage with guinea pigs. The cage should not be open at the top, because mice can climb out. Contrary to popular

Dogs and guinea pigs can sometimes become good friends.

19

belief, rats are also companionable partners, who will not harm the guinea pig's young. But, some guinea pigs cannot stand rats and will chase them away.

Golden hamster: Experiences vary. Some people say that guinea pigs cannot defend themselves against hamsters' aggressiveness. On the other hand, friendships have been known to develop.

Turtle: It's better not to put a turtle in with a guinea pig; guinea pigs will try to nibble on the turtles.

Birds: Birds will swipe the guinea pig's food. Budgerigars are fond of nibbling at guinea pigs' ears. Parrots and larger parakeets become jealous and will peck the little creature.

Guinea Pigs and Children

Guinea pigs are ideal for children, since they possess all the qualities a child looks for in a pet. They are sociable, like to be petted, and the more attention they get, the livelier and brighter they are. In the process, children learn how to deal with the animal in a responsible, natural way.

Parents should assume some share of the responsibility. Look into the cage now and then, to check that the guinea pig is still bustling about in a lively way and eating regularly. A change in behavior usually indicates a health problem, which children may be unable to detect right away.

Note: More than one guinea pig has been squeezed to death by children out of sheer love. The problem is that the guinea pig does not resist, scratch or bite and cannot jump down as nimbly as a cat. Make all of this clear to your child in advance, to spare him or her the experience of possibly causing the animal's death.

Vacation Care

Before buying a guinea pig, you also need to give careful thought to the question of its care while you are on vacation or absent for some other reason.

Leaving it at home: With enough water, dry food, and hay, your guinea pig can stay alone in its cage quite easily for one or two days. For a longer absence, you need a dependable person who will come into your home once or twice a day, give the guinea pig food, clean the cage, and also have some time to cuddle and play. It is essential to leave behind instructions for care and the

Guinea pigs generally get along very well together and they always have lots to "talk" about.

address of your veterinarian. Pet sitters are becoming increasingly available and offer their services for a fee. They usually advertise their services in the classified sections of newspapers.

Taking it along: If you want to take your guinea pig along, it has to be appropriately "bundled" during the trip. If the trip is only a short one, a sturdy cardboard box with air holes will suffice. A better choice is a travel cage made of plastic, with an air-permeable cover and convenient handles. Ask your hotel or

21

motel in advance whether your pet will be welcome. When traveling abroad, contact the consulate—well ahead of time—to find out what procedures are required for crossing the border.

Note: Guinea pigs can be affected by a sudden change of climate. Before your trip, you need to consider whether you want to subject yourself and your pet to this kind of stress.

Boarding it: Neighbors, relatives, or friends may offer their services here. Children often are quite enthusiastic about taking care of an animal for a few weeks. Notices posted in a nearby pet store or on the supermarket bulletin board are also good sources for possible boarding.

Traveling with the Guinea Pig

Keep the following pointers in mind and your guinea pig will remain unharmed in a train or car trip:

Equipment:

■ Cover a cardboard box with a thick layer of plastic and bedding, so that no urine can seep through. Guinea pigs' urine has an unpleasant smell and will leave stains. Of

Will a Guinea Pig Become Tame?

Your little friend has finally arrived and it's hiding out in its little house. And you would so much like to take it in your arms and feed it tidbits. But that's not easily done right away. First of all, you must gain the animal's confidence. Basically, that isn't hard. After all, guinea pigs are very social animals. In nature, they live together in small groups, look for food together, and always have lots to tell each other. As a domestic pet, the guinea pig hasn't lost this behavior. As soon as it has grown accustomed to your voice and your scent, it will forget its shyness, let you pet it, and eat out of your hand.

Accommodations:

■ Under no circumstances should your pet be transported in a closed trunk on a car trip. Heat accumulates in the cramped space there, causing the guinea pig needless suffering and possibly even resulting in its death. Of course, it is all right to put the cardboard box or travel cage into the open rear luggage area of a station wagon or onto the back seat of your car. Cover it loosely with a cloth or a blanket, to protect the guinea pig from drafts and direct sunlight. When you stop for a break, park the car in the shade (caution, the sun moves!), and don't stay away from the car too long. If you leave it parked for a fairly long time, the air inside will become stifling, which could also affect the guinea pig badly.

■ Keep your guinea pig in the compartment with you on the train. It would certainly be frightened to death in the baggage car. As in the car, protect your pet against drafts and direct sunlight.

course, straw must also be put into the travel cage.

■ Hay and water in the drinking water container are all the provisions your pet needs. On a longer trip, keep a supply of fresh foods such as fruit or lettuce. A few carrots or other root crops will also be welcomed by your guinea pig.

Children will carry their guinea pig more securely if they grasp it with both hands and hold it against their chest.

The Law and the Pet Owner

Believe it or not, even such unproblematic animals as guinea pigs can give rise to problems. It is advisable to find out in advance what your rights as a pet owner are. Sometimes there are confrontations that can be settled only in the courts. The most common legal issues are summarized below.

If You Live in a Rented Apartment

Before you decide to get a guinea pig, you should read over your lease. If there is any doubt whether pets are allowed in your building, it is advisable to get written permission from your landlord.

If your lease contains no provisions concerning pets, you can assume that pets may be kept in your rented apartment. Today, having a pet is usually considered to be part of one's life-style and therefore part of the use of the rented apartment as stipulated, as long as the pet causes no disturbance. This is generally true, all the more so if small rodents such as guinea pigs are involved. By virtue of their species and nature, these animals are incapable of disturbing domestic peace and security.

They have no annoying odors, nor do they make noises that could disturb fellow tenants. These animals are also incapable of causing substantial damage to the apartment.

Therefore the tenant does not need special permission to keep a guinea pig. Problems arise only if one or two guinea pigs turn into an entire breeding group with a large number of animals. The extent to which domestic peace and security might or might not be disturbed must be considered.

If used cage bedding smells, this material must be disposed of in accordance with regulations, so that no other residents of the building are bothered.

One or two guinea pigs do not make enough noise to disturb your neighbors.

Owner-Occupied Apartments and Communities

Policies vary widely from community to community (e.g., many senior citizen communities will allow you to join the community with an existing pet and forbid you to acquire any new pets while a condominium complex may not let you join their community at all if you already own a pet). It is therefore wise to find out what the policies are for your particular community.

A general prohibition against keeping guinea pigs (or any pet) in an owner-occupied apartment can effectively be adopted only by covenant, usually through a majority decision of the apartment owners.

Animal Owner's Liability

If an animal causes injury to a person or property, the animal's owner is always liable.

This is an absolute liability; that is, the animal owner is liable even if he or she personally has not been negligent. These principles apply not only to large or dangerous animals, but also to a guinea pig that bites a child. The injured party may be held partially to blame if the animal is provoked. Under some circumstances the contributory negligence can be so great that the animal owner's liability is wholly or partially diminished.

Such situations, however, can usually be avoided by providing close supervision when your pet "entertains" visitors.

Sales Contract

Everyone who purchases a guinea pig enters into a contract of sale with the seller.

This contract does not have to be drawn up in written form, since oral contracts are also legally binding. If, after the guinea pig has been handed over to the purchaser, the animal is found to be defective (that is, diseased), the buyer may be able to withdraw from the contract or reduce the purchase price.

This presupposes, however, that the animal already was ill when it came into the buyer's possession. The onset of the illness is very difficult to determine, particularly with infectious diseases. Usually only specialized veterinarians are able to clarify these issues.

Guinea pigs are not considered to be particularly bright. They make up for this, however, by being very social.

25

Where to Get a Guinea Pig

A guinea pig should not only look good, but be healthy as well. That is why it is important to go to the right place to buy your pet and to keep your wits about you.

Domestic or Purebred Guinea Pig?

Your child has fallen in love with a friend's guinea pig and now he or she absolutely has to have one of those sweet little animals too. Your son or daughter also knows that young guinea pigs are available in the nearby pet store. The child's heart has already been lost to a parti-colored, checkered guinea pig with a shaggy, wiry coat, because its hair stands on end in such a cute way and one side of its face looks like it was dipped in black ink.

Your children and many other guinea pig fanciers are concerned only with the little, squealing bundle of fur. They don't care whether it's a domestic or a purebred guinea pig. Those interested in breeding guinea pigs, however, have to be on the lookout for animals that display the suitable characteristics of the breed. (See Planned Breeding of Guinea Pigs, p. 78.)

Guinea pigs not only multiply "like rabbits," they also display some of the same features as far as breeding is concerned. If all you want is a small, squealing bundle of fur, you need not worry about deciding between a domestic guinea pig and a purebred.

■ Domestic guinea pig is the term applied to all animals that were not bred according to certain rules.

■ They are of one color or spotted, have ears that stick out, crooked feet, whorls in the wrong place, hair that's too long or too short, in short, they display "faults," which make them unsuitable for planned breeding.

■ Purebred guinea pigs are distinguished by definitely established criteria for the appearance and characteristics of a variety of colors and hair types. This didn't happen overnight, but represents the results of many years of patient breeding efforts.

Where to Find the Kind of Guinea Pig You Want

Pet stores have guinea pigs in many

A three-colored gold-agouti, red-white.

Bright eyes, a smooth coat, and a healthy appetite are good indicators as to whether a guinea pig is thriving.

colors and with different types of coats. Such stores are making more of an effort to offer purebred guinea pigs.

Take your time about making the purchase, and take a good look at the store. Unfortunately, this line of business has its share of shrewd profiteers, for whom the proper care of guinea pigs is not a matter of great concern. Good pet store dealers do not house their guinea pigs in overcrowded, cramped quarters; they keep the cage and food and water bowls clean and are concerned with the animals' well-being. In addition, they will give you detailed advice about making your selection.

Note: If you ever have young guinea pigs that need new homes, entrust them only to a pet store dealer whose premises you have closely inspected in advance.

27

You can find just what you want with a breeder. It is best to gather information at a guinea pig show before you go to a breeder. This will give you a good overview of the assortment of available breeds. You can get more detailed information from the American Cavy Breeders Association (see Useful Addresses, page 125).

Note: The cost of a guinea pig varies widely. Make inquiries in advance to protect yourself from paying outrageous prices. Young guinea pigs may be offered in the classified section of newspapers. If the owner seems very concerned about where and how the animal will be kept, you can be certain that it comes from a "good stable."

There is often someone in your neighborhood who has young guinea pigs to give away. The bulletin board in your veterinarian's office or local supermarket may also prove useful: you may post a "Guinea Pig Wanted" notice or find a "Guinea Pigs Available" notice there.

Let the Buyer Beware

You probably already have your new housemate: Usually people don't buy a pet owner's manual until they purchase the pet or run into problems. My advice, then, will come a little late. Never mind, there may be a next time.

Whether you are planning to buy your new housemate or get it free from someone, you still need to take plenty of time in making your selection. Direct your attention to the table on page 31.

■ It is best to choose a young animal, approximately five to six weeks old. At this age it still is markedly smaller than adult animals and weighs between 10.5 and 17.6 ounces (300–600 g). A female that is over two months old may already be pregnant (see page 82).

■ Guinea pigs are sociable creatures. Watch closely to see how the animal you choose behaves with its fellows. Is it frisky and cheerful and eager to play with them, or does it sit listlessly in a corner and keep itself aloof? The latter behavior is a symptom of disease.

■ Take a look at its coat. Heavy shedding, a thin coat, and bare patches are signs of disease or old age.

■ Examine the guinea pig's teeth—in the pet store, with the dealer's help. If the teeth

How Do Offspring Get Here?

Your friend's guinea pigs have had young ones and she's given you one of them. Eight weeks later three animals are scampering about in the cage. How is that possible? After it's only five weeks old a female guinea is already capable of giving birth.

Obviously your friend waited more than five weeks and the animal wasn't separated from its parents in time to avoid getting pregnant.

That's how your guinea pig coupled with the male and came to you pregnant.

Guinea pigs get along well with dwarf rabbits— sometimes even better than with other guinea pigs.

are poorly positioned, you can count on problems at some later date (see Tooth Check, page 30).

■ Pay attention to the feet and claws as well. If the guinea pig limps, it may have an inflammation.

Note: Take some of the nest material from the pet store cage home with you. That will make it easier for the guinea pig to adjust to its new surroundings. Pine wood shavings are by far the best!

Good Health Is Important

When guinea pigs are properly fed and cared for and get enough exercise, they seldom get sick. You can help to keep your pet in good health by performing the examinations described below, periodically. Appropriate care entails enabling the animal to live in a way befitting its species. If it ever sits around and seems bored and listless, that does not necessarily indicate a health problem.

Tooth Check

A guinea pig's teeth, like its claws, regrow throughout its life. If they are not worn down sufficiently, they become overly long and get in the animal's way when it eats, until finally it is no longer able to eat at all. Then they have to be cut or filed down by the veterinarian (see pages 59 and 60). To check your pet's teeth, proceed as follows: open its mouth carefully (see Drawing 1); place one hand under its belly for support, and with your other hand exert a slight pressure at the back of its head, behind the teeth—the guinea pig will automatically open its mouth.

The rodent teeth, or front incisors, of the upper and lower jaws must contact each other so that they can wear down properly.

The molars should bite together. Sometimes they become too sharp-edged as they wear down and injure the cheek and tongue. Use your finger to test for sharp edges.

Anal Check

Accumulations of feces around the anus are a sign of diarrhea, which can have a number of different causes: e.g., improper diet, intestinal parasites, infections, or viral diseases. Diarrhea—particularly if it persists for any length of time—is always an alarm signal, and it should be kept under close observation (see page 73). It is best to take your pet to the veterinarian. Use a damp cloth to clean the sticky anal region (see Drawing 2).

Skin Check

Checking skin regularly is important, too, because many skin diseases can be transferred to humans (see Drawing 2 and page 70). Constant scratching of the same area, fearfulness, and restlessness are clear indications that something is the matter.

1 The teeth must be properly aligned.

2 Examine the skin for parasites or fungal infections.

3 Look for traces of mites (mite deposits, residues) when checking the ears.

Selecting the Right Guinea Pig

	Healthy Guinea Pig	Sick Guinea Pig
Body	Well-padded all around	Flanks caved in
Coat	Thick and shiny	Shaggy, thin, with bare patches
Eyes	Bright and a bit moist, with no discharge	Too dry, lids stuck together, inflamed
Nose	Dry and warm	Crusted, with discharge
Ears	Clean	Dark brown crusts, increased scratching
Anal area	Clean	Smeared with feces
Feet	Undersides bare and smooth	Inflamed; claws growing in different directions
Behavior	Alert, frisky, "talks" with other members of its species	Listless, apathetic

Note: If the guinea pig has diarrhea (recognizable by the sticky hair around the anus), do not buy, or accept as a gift, any other animal from the same cage. Diarrhea can be a symptom of contagious bacterial or viral infections.

Parasites such as lice or mites can be recognized by inflamed areas and hair loss.

Diseases caused by skin fungi, such as microsporosis, are recognized by circular, bare patches, in some cases with thick crusts or scales. Often the hair falls out in these places. Itching is not usually acute. Your guinea pig may also be suffering from allergies or hormonal imbalances. All these diseases can be properly treated only by a veterinarian.

Ear Check

Guinea pigs' ears can be affected or become inflamed indirectly by ear mites, and externally by a skin disease. Such problems can be detected early and treated immediately through regular checkups (see Drawing 3). The symptoms include increased scratching at the ear. Brown crusts and an unpleasant odor are also symptoms of ear mites. Reddened and inflamed skin in the ear canal (shine a flashlight inside) is a sign of an ear inflammation. Small bare patches on the ears are indications of a skin disease. Consult a veterinarian immediately if you notice any of these symptoms listed above.

31

Profile of the Guinea Pig

The breeding of guinea pigs has been common for many years in the United States and Europe. Shows are also organized and prizes awarded to the best animals in the country.

Characteristics of Purebred Guinea Pigs

A purebred guinea pig must display certain characteristics that are set forth by a standard commission and judged at shows. The following guidelines apply to purebred guinea pigs:

Body: Well-muscled and powerful, but not plump, heavy, or fat. Broad and short in type, with well-rounded hindquarters and with no tail.

Legs: Straight and powerful. Four toes and claws on each of the front paws, three on the hind paws.

Head: Well-developed, broad between eyes and ears, nose arched, muzzle nicely rounded, with well-developed cheeks.

Eyes: Large and clear, slightly protruding.

Ears: Fleshy and standing out horizontally, shaped like rose petals, somewhat wavy in the center and slightly drooping.

Size and weight: Between 8 and 13 in. (22 and 35 cm). A full-grown animal should weigh between 32 and 42 oz. (900 and 1200 g).

Coat: The quality of the various hair types is judged.

Special breed characteristics: Various colors and types of markings.

What Is a Breed Standard?

The breed standard is the term applied to the description of the "ideal" member of a breed.

At shows, purebred guinea pigs are judged according to the breed standard. On the following pages I describe how the breeds of guinea pigs must look, in terms of their coat (color, markings), claws, and eyes, in order to conform to the standard.

Breeds

There were only three breeds when guinea pigs were first shown in the United States under the Standard of the American Rabbit Breeders Association (ARBA). Today there are eleven recognized breeds, with more on the way. The eleven breeds recognized by the American Cavy Breed-

Three (little) bundles of fur: sheltie, three-colored (left), Holland angora, red-white (center) and alpaca, red-white (right).

ers Association are as follows: Abyssinian, Abyssinian Satin, American, American Satin, Peruvian, Peruvian Satin, Silkie, Silkie Satin, Teddy, Teddy Satin, and White Crested.

Color Varieties

A guinea pig with a uniform, basic color, evenly distributed over the entire body, is called a color variety.

■ *Agouti*

This technical term for "wild" colors—grizzled gray or dark brown—refers to a coat color that most closely approaches that of the guinea pig's wild ancestors. The coloring is produced by the presence of two to three bands, of light and dark colors on each individual hair shaft, with the tip of the hair always darkest. This is known as ticking. Stripes, patches, and brindling are not permissible with this color.

Golden agouti: Black with red bars. Eyes dark. Claws black.

Gray agouti (wild color): Black with buff bars. Eyes dark. Claws black.

Silver agouti: Black with silver gray bars. Eyes dark. Claws black.

Cinnamon agouti: Cinnamon with silver white bars. Eyes ruby. Claws brown.

Salmon agouti: Golden with lilac bars. Eyes red. Claws horn-colored.

■ *Self (or single) colored*

Black: Deep black. Eyes dark. Claws black.

Chocolate: Like bitter chocolate. Eyes ruby. Claws dark.

Lilac: Light blue, with pink sheen. Eyes red. Claws horn-colored.

Beige: Dark cream color, with gray sheen. Eyes red. Nails horn-colored.

Red: Very dark, warm red (like Irish setter). Eyes dark. Claws dark horn-color.

Golden: Warm orange. Eyes red. Claws horn-colored.

Buff: Dark ocher. Eyes dark. Claws horn-colored.

Cream: Light cream color. Eyes dark. Claws horn-colored.

White: Pure white. Eyes dark, blue, or red. Claws light-colored.

Marked (or multicolored) Varieties

In multicolored animals, the various colors are distributed in certain patterns over the coat. These are called marked varieties.

Brindle: Red and black hairs evenly distributed over the body. Eyes dark. Claws dark.

English crested, black. The rosette on the head is the same color as the body.

Normal hair, tortoisehshell, and white, in the color combination chocolate-red-white.

Normal hair, Holland (Dutch) guinea pig. Hind quarters and "cheeks" have the same color.

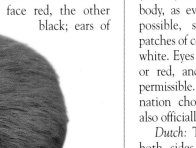

Tortoiseshell: Sharply delineated red and black fields of color (like a checkerboard), distributed very evenly. Eyes dark. Claws dark.

Japanese: One half of the face red, the other black; ears of the opposite color. Trunk banded in red and black (zebra marking). Eyes dark. Claws dark.

Tortoiseshell and white (tricolor): On either side of the body, as evenly distributed as possible, sharply delineated patches of color: black, red, and white. Eyes may be either dark or red, and white claws are permissible. The color combination chocolate-red-white is also officially recognized.

Dutch: The same color on both sides of the body (in between, a white blaze) and on the lower third of the body, the remainder is white, and both hind feet are white

35

toward the tip. In black, chocolate, red, and agouti. Eyes dark. Claws colorless.

Himalayan/Russian: White with dark mask, ideally pear-shaped and extending to the eye line—that is, covering only the nose. Ears and feet also must be dark. Permissible in black and chocolate. Eyes red. Claws dark.

Abyssinian Guinea Pig

Also known as the rosette or whorled guinea pig, it is characterized by its unusual coat. The coat is shaggy and wiry, and it stands stiffly away from the body. At least eight rosettes (ten is the ideal number) are distributed uniformly over the entire body; the ridges between the rosettes should stand up like brushes and be so situated that an

Rosette, brindle. Red and black hairs are evenly distributed.

attractive double effect is achieved. As a result, the animal has a comical, shaggy look, and it is sometimes called the shaggy-haired guinea pig. The colors and combinations of colors recognized officially are red, black, white, tricolor, brindle, tortoiseshell, broken (color evenly distributed), black roan (distribution of hairs approximately 1:1 white with black), red roan (1:1 white with red), and mixed roan (1:1 white, black, and red).

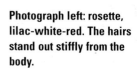

Photograph left: rosette, lilac-white-red. The hairs stand out stiffly from the body.

Texel, red. The hairs are long and wavy in a corkscrew pattern.

Rex, sepia-white. The coat is short, fine and soft textured.

Texel

The texel guinea pig is a cross between the Sheltie and the rex. The hair on its head is short and tightly curled; on the body it is long and curly or wavy. The colors red-and-white and red are officially recognized.

Rex

Rex guinea pigs, like rex cats, have wavy or curly hair that is short, fine, and soft-textured. The colors red-and-white and buff are officially recognized. Only the coat, however, is judged.

English and American Crested

These animals are smooth-haired, with a single rosette that has to be located precisely in the middle of the forehead, in the rectangular area between the eyes and the ears. It must have only one center.

■ *English crested:* The rosette is the same color as the body, and these colors are recognized officially: agouti, all monotone varieties, and white.

■ *American crested:* Here the rosette is white, and only the following colors are officially recognized: black, red, golden, and buff.

37

Satin

In fact, they are members of the smooth-haired category, but because of their unusually silky, shiny hair these guinea pigs have been recognized as a separate breed. Their coat is finer and thicker than that of "normal" guinea pigs. The satiny sheen—which, incidentally, is the most important factor in the judging—causes the color to seem more intense. When the light hits it, the coat should really shine. These colors are admissible: red, golden, buff, cream, and white.

Originally bred only as the smooth-haired satin, there are now also other coat types: Abyssinian, English and American Crested, Peruvian, Sheltie, Coronet, and Teddy. Soon satin varieties of all the other guinea pig breeds will be available as well.

Satin, one-colored (monochrome) red. A particularly attractive specimen.

English crested satin, monochrome cream. The tuft (crest) of hair on the forehead is of the same color.

American crested. This crested guinea pig has a white rosette on its head.

Long-haired Guinea Pig (Peruvian or "Silky")

This type has long, thick, shiny hair, which has a silky, soft feel especially in young animals.

Satin, Himalaya. The black spots get darker in cold weather.

Because of a part on the back, the hair hangs like a mane on both sides of the body. The hair on the hindquarters forms a train. On the head sits a whorl which creates a thick, long fringe.

Two symmetrical rosettes on the hips make the coat look like it has a part in it. A whorl on the head makes it appear to have bangs. The officially recognized colors are red, black, white, tricolor, tortoiseshell, and red broken or black broken (black and white).

39

Sheltie

The hair is long, thick, and shiny, as with the longhaired guinea pig. The longer they grow, the softer and silkier they are to the touch. A dense part on the back causes the hairs on the shoulder and the sides to slope down like a mane. The train spreads out like a fan. The Sheltie has no bangs—the hairs grow back. But it does have sideburns.

The officially recognized colors are black, red, white, tortoiseshell, tricolor, and black broken or red broken.

The coronet, a crested Peruvian, is not yet recognized by us.

Sheltie cream-black-white.

Longhair, white-lilac, a particularly unusual color.

Breeds Not Yet Officially Recognized

Coronet: Longhaired variant of the crested; that is, a Peruvian with a thatch (whorl) on its forehead.

Teddy: A breed developed in America; it looks like the rex but is not genetically identical.

Alpaca: A texel with whorls, bred by crossing longhaired and rex guinea pigs.

Merino: A crested texel, bred by crossing the coronet and the rex.

Holland angora, red-white. The number and position of the whorls are precisely prescribed.

Proper Care and Grooming

Guinea pigs are good-natured and lovable. Frisky and cheerful, they hop around their cage and squeal with delight at feeding time. Make sure to provide your pet with appropriate housing, a nutritionally balanced diet, and loving care. Then your little companion will lead a long and happy life.

All it takes is a treat to get your guinea pig to perform all sorts of gymnastics.

Equipment and Housing

Guinea pigs are not demanding "tenants." All they need is a roomy cage, enough bedding, and a little house into which they can retreat for privacy.

The Cage: A Happy Home

"You don't need anything special for a guinea pig; a cardboard box will do just fine," I often hear people say. Although this comment reveals a great deal of ignorance, there is some truth in it.

It is true that guinea pigs have no characteristic patterns of behavior that make special housing necessary. They do not climb and do acrobatics like hamsters; they can jump into the air, of course, but by no means so high as rabbits; nor are they bent on "breaking out" of their quarters at all costs. Guinea pigs, therefore, make no great demands—but that does not mean that you can neglect them completely. After all, you want them to stay healthy and frisky and feel happy in your home; that is

A ladder invites climbing and keeps the guinea pig in shape when it goes to eat.

If you provide a rough bottom surface, the guinea pig's claws will wear down naturally, quite as they do in nature.

only possible with the right kind of accommodations. You need to give your pet as much room to move around in as possible.

The cage floor should be at least 16 × 32 inches (40 × 80 cm). The best type of cage has a plastic bottom tray and a removable top. The bottom tray should be 4 to 6 inches (10–15 cm) high, so that the bedding is less likely to be kicked out. An upper part with bars that can be raised from above or on the side is useful, but does have the disadvantage of the straw being able to fly out. The plastic hood has the advantage of affording the guinea pig a good view of its surroundings and the straw is not easily kicked out. Nevertheless, it can sometimes get too hot underneath it.

Cardboard boxes are *not* suitable for guinea pig housing.

You can transport guinea pigs in them, but only for a limited amount of time. If you leave the animal in such a box, the cardboard will soon begin to disintegrate because it is saturated with urine, and it will quickly be gnawed to pieces. Wooden boxes are also not advisable, since they are hard to clean and also become urine-soaked.

A Little House to Sleep In

Guinea pigs like to sleep with a "roof over their heads." A good choice for that purpose is a small wooden box that suits the animal's size and has a hole cut into it. You can find these little wooden houses in various sizes in pet stores. Wood is preferable, since the guinea pig can sharpen its teeth on it.

Tips for do-it-yourselfers: You can also build a house yourself, keeping the following rules in mind:

■ Wood such as spruce, pine, or larch is preferable to chipboard or rough fiberboard.
■ Don't fasten the boards together with metal staples; the guinea pig could injure itself by nibbling them. It is better to use fairly large U-staples made of steel; they cannot be gnawed out so easily.
■ If you want to use glue, use a nontoxic glue. Let the house air out for a few days after it has been glued. Glued houses can be reinforced with strips of wood at the corners.

Hayrack

A rack, or crib, for the hay is a necessity. Naturally, you can simply lay the hay on the floor of the cage. However, if there are several animals in the cage, the hay will quickly get soiled with feces and urine.

Two feed racks are preferable, since the same problems arise with green feed. Usually hayracks come with the cage when you buy it, but they also can be purchased separately in pet stores. A hinged

The hay will stay clean and appetizing in a food tray.

The animal will quickly get used to the nipple tip of the gravity flow bottle.

The salt lick shouldn't be on the floor.

A flower pot serves as a cave and cinder blocks serve as a stairway—that's all you need to make the cage "interesting."

wooden lid that covers the top of the hayracks is very useful. The guinea pig cannot climb into the rack or pull it down. Even better, it can sit on the hinged lid, which it loves to do.

Water Dispenser

A gravity-flow bottle, which you can hang on the cage wire, is the best choice for drinking water, since water in an open dish quickly gets full of feces and bedding. The glass or plastic bottle should be equipped with a ball valve to keep the water from dripping into the cage. The guinea pig will quickly learn to help itself.

Claw-Sharpening Stone

Guinea pigs need to walk over a hard, rough surface (see page 59) to wear their claws down. A lava stone is a good choice.

Food Dish

The food dish must be sturdy and should not tip over. Bowls made of glazed clay or porcelain are very suitable; plastic dishes overturn easily. Don't get too large a bowl either, since some animals will sit right down in it. An automated food dispenser should contain no more than a day's ration; otherwise, the guinea pig will eat nonstop.

A Plastic Tub as a Guinea Pig Home

If you would like to postpone the purchase of a large and expensive cage for the time being, you can substitute a laundry basket or a child's bathtub that is no longer in use. The container must be approximately the same size as a cage. These alternatives, however, should not become a permanent solution.

Advantages
■ The high sides help the guinea pig help feel more secure.
■ The straw is unlikely to be kicked out.
■ The tub or laundry basket is easy to clean and wash.

Disadvantages
■ The food tray and water dispenser are hard to attach.
■ The high sides isolate the pet from its surroundings.
■ It is not protected from cats, for example, which could present a serious threat.

Note: Since the guinea pig will need a house to sleep in,

you can solve two problems at once. Attach the hayrack and water dispenser to the house; the guinea pig can jump on top of the house and look over the side of the tub.

A Guinea Pig House for Do-it-yourselfers

Guinea pig fanciers who are handy have an easy solution to the housing problem. They can make a little house themselves and give free rein to their imagination.

A homemade residence can be equipped with everything that characterizes the guinea pig's natural habitat in the wild: places to hide, little hollows, some high ground for keeping a lookout, stones to sharpen its claws naturally, and branches to gnaw on. By adding a second level, you can offer your guinea pig two features: a place to hide down below and a lookout area up above.

Here's how to plan your pet's home:
■ *Size:* At least as large as a store-bought cage, (32 × 16 × 16 inches [80 × 40 × 40 cm]). Of course, you can make a larger surface area.
■ *Material:* Waterproof, untreated natural wood boards 3/4 inch (20 mm) thick. Do

T I P

When grooming the coats of longhaired animals you need a broad-toothed comb to disentangle the hair, a wire brush with plastic caps for thorough brushing, and a soft baby brush for the sheen.

The hollow piece of wood is an ideal sleeping house and the animal can chew on it to its heart's content.

not use plywood sheets, since they contain formaldehyde.

■ *Bottom insert:* A pan made of plastic (cat litter box, available in pet stores) or sheet metal; untreated wood becomes saturated with urine.

■ *Upper level:* The platform should be about 6 inches (15 cm) high and cover up to one-third of the surface area.

■ *Sides:* Three sides should be 16 inches (40 cm) high; make the fourth side, opposite the upper tier, 4 to 6 inches (10–15 cm) high, and cover it with wire mesh. You have to be able to open the fourth side with a hinge at the top or at one side. Then you can pull out the bottom insert for cleaning, and the guinea pig also can go in and out

49

alone during its exercise period.

■ *Roof:* If the cage is 16 inches (40 cm) high, a roof is needed over the upper tier only.

■ *Accessories:* A flat rock, placed in front of the upper tier so that the guinea pig has to go over it to get onto the platform. Branches to nibble and gnaw. A flowerpot, placed on its side, to hide in or climb on. An cement pipe (available where builders' supplies are sold) to crawl into.

The Right Bedding

Coarse sawdust is cheap and easy to get. To absorb the odor, place a layer of cat litter beneath the bedding. Some guinea pig owners advise against doing so, since young animals in particular may nibble at the cat litter, which can make them sick. The same objection arises if you put a thick layer of newspaper, instead of cat litter, underneath. Provided the animals merely gnaw at the newspaper and do not eat any of it, no

A roomy cage, along with a daily free run in the home, is all a guinea pig needs to be content.

Guinea pigs like to sleep with a "roof over their heads."

Why Do Guinea Pigs Like to Go into Caves?

Have you already noticed how many times a day your guinea pig slips into its little sleeping house? Yet it doesn't really get that much sleep. It often holes up in it because it feels so thoroughly safe there, for guinea pigs are flight animals, which means they don't defend themselves against enemies but instead run away from them and hide in their caves. As domestic pets they've still kept this habit, although at home with you, there's really no danger at all.

harm is done. But if they swallow too many of the scraps, you have to remove the newspaper, since the printer's ink may harm them.

Straw is something that guinea pigs are very fond of; they rustle around in it and play hide-and-seek, but they love to nibble on it. Straw is sold in pet stores, but if you need more, you can get it from a farmer.

Organic bedding for small animals, available in pet stores, is highly absorbent and free of harmful substances. On the other hand, it is somewhat more expensive.

Note: With longhaired breeds, use sawdust only as a bottom layer and place a thick layer of straw on top of it. The wood shavings get caught in the long hair and cause ugly mats (see page 57).

The Right Place for the Cage

A guinea pig needs to be treated as "one of the family." It is a highly sociable animal, and an extremely isolated location would run counter to its need for contact. That does not mean, though, that its surroundings should be chaotic. Guinea pigs dislike too much

noise and loud music, since they are easily frightened. Moreover, they have much keener hearing than humans and are affected by sounds that we cannot even hear.

The best location is a bright, not overly warm room that is free of drafts. Drafts are very harmful to guinea pigs. Since there are usually drafts at floor level, the cage should be elevated. Place it on a table that does not wobble or on a chest of drawers. Your pet will have a good view from such a position as well.

Indoor Exercise

Guinea pigs need to train their physical and sensory capabilities; otherwise, they will become dull pets that just sit around in their cage—as so many people think they do. If you have ever seen guinea pigs in hot pursuit of one another, you know how much they need exercise. Give your pet the opportunity to fulfill that need.

Note the following:

■ There should be no valuable rugs and furniture in the room; they might be gnawed and will become dirty.

■ Electric cords should be out of reach. Guinea pigs like to nibble on them, and the results

Dangers for Guinea Pigs

Danger	Source of Danger	Avoiding the Danger
Falling	Balcony	Secure with wire mesh or boards.
	Table	Do not let animals run free without supervision.
Pinching	Doors	Do not open or close without looking.
Heat stroke	Sun, heating units	Never let the cage stand in the direct sunlight or near a heating units.
Electric shock	Electrical cords	Conceal wiring; do not leave cords lying around; unplug cords when guinea pig is out of its cage.
Burns	Hot objects	Don't let guinea pig out near stove, toaster, or burning candles. Cigarettes and butts are dangerous, too.
Poison	Poisonous houseplants	Don't keep poisonous plants in the guinea pig's environment.
	Stained or lacquered wood	Use nontoxic materials.
Injuries	Human feet	Be careful when your pet is out of its cage.

Running free in the home is important for the guinea pig.

can be fatal. Telephone cords are also a temptation.

■ Put a shallow bowl of straw in the room to serve as a guinea pig potty (see page 104).

■ Don't leave newspapers and books lying around. Guinea pigs are real little devils, and they love paper. Loose edges of wallpaper are not safe either.

■ Provide your pets with an environment that offers plenty of variety, with nooks and crannies, elevated places (an up-ended flowerpot, for example), and little obstacles to jump over (see Great Ideas for Playing, page 108).

Summer Vacation on the Balcony

If you have a roomy balcony, you can let your guinea pig share it with you. Arrange your pet's area so that it is comfortable from spring through late fall. Of course, when the outside temperature drops below 50°F (10°C) you have to take your pet indoors. Keep the following in mind:

Safety: The guinea pig can squeeze through balcony railings or under balustrades that don't reach all the way to the floor, and plunge to its death. Secure the balcony railings with chicken wire.

The chicken wire should rest firmly on the floor and reach about 16 inches (40 cm) high. Cover balustrades that are open at the bottom with wooden boards.

Note: If you have railings, put up a board as well; it will prevent drafts and also will give your pet something to gnaw on.

Protection: The balcony needs to be protected against wind, rain, and direct sunlight. Cover the cold concrete floor with old carpet squares or a natural grass mat to keep the guinea pig from catching cold.

Cats: A balcony at ground-floor level may be accessible to cats—with tragic consequences. Secure the balcony with a fine-mesh screen if your landlord doesn't object.

Changes in temperature: You have to accustom your pet to temperature changes when you take the guinea pig from indoors to outdoors, or vice versa. Otherwise, it will catch cold. Begin by putting it outdoors during the warm midday hours and bring it back inside at night. Do not bring it into a heated room immediately during the fall. The animal will feel happiest

at a temperature of 64 to 68°F (18–20°C).

Feeding: The guinea pig must be given fresh food and water twice a day.

Overnight: To spend the night out on the balcony, the guinea pig needs its little house (see page 46). Don't forget to put out the shallow bowl of straw for use as a toilet.

Outdoor Enclosure (Pen)

If you have a yard, you can let your pet out regularly for exercise or even set up permanent quarters for it there, especially if you own several guinea pigs. Their bond with humans, in this case, however, will be less close, because life as part of a pack will completely satisfy the animal's need for contact.

Enclosure: Ready-made enclosures are available in pet stores, or you can also make one yourself. First, build four sturdy frames with wooden stakes. Cover the frames with

An open air enclosure with a little house for protection and wire mesh fencing will provide a nice area for many guinea pigs.

Why Do Guinea Pigs Chatter with Their Teeth?

If your little pet does that, it's not because it's cold but because it feels threatened. Maybe you grabbed it too hard without noticing and it got scared. At first you'll hear a growl. That doesn't mean that it wants to attack you. Instead it's saying: please don't do anything to me. If you don't understand that, the guinea pig will start chattering his teeth furiously. If you still don't understand, then it might really bite your finger.

chicken wire and hinge them together, remember that the enclosure needs to be at least one square yard (1 m²). The top should be covered with chicken wire to keep other animals from threatening the guinea pigs.

Safety: Because guinea pigs dig very little, the enclosure does not have to be anchored in the ground. Nonetheless, it needs to be securely and firmly fixed in place, so that the guinea pigs cannot get out and rats and weasels cannot get in.

Protection: Guinea pigs need shelter in their enclosure. This not only protects them from rain, sun, and wind, but is also a refuge from their enemies and a place to hide when they get scared. It should be at least the size of the cage they live in—about 32 × 16 × 16 inches (80 × 40 × 40 cm). Several guinea pigs, will need a correspondingly larger house. To build it, use ¾-inch (20 mm) thick, waterproof, untreated natural wood boards, a window, and a roof that can be removed or folded back—so that you can remove the old straw. On the front side, cut a 4 to 6 inch (10–15 cm) entryway, with a sliding door or a hinged flap, so that it can be closed. Alternatively, hang a burlap bag over the entryway. Cover the roof with tarpaper. The roof should slant on the windward side and jut out far enough to protect the food and water bowls below it. Put one or two racks inside the shelter for hay.

Overwintering Outdoors?

Since guinea pigs live at elevations of some 13,000 feet (4000 m) in the Andes, where it gets very cold, you may be able to let them spend the winters outdoors as well. Check with your veterinarian on this. The only requirement is that you keep the animals outdoors all through the summer. Do not wait until fall to put them outside. In addition, make the following arrangements:

■ Protect the stall from drafts and insulate it with styrofoam; place plenty of straw and hay inside it.

■ If it gets very cold outside, drape the stall with blankets at night. You might also cover the openings with styrofoam.

■ Pad a thick layer of hay or straw inside the little house.

Note: Newborn guinea pigs will be better off indoors.

The Well-Groomed Guinea Pig

Guinea pigs that are healthy and happy groom themselves at great length and keep their coats scrupulously clean. Be sure to clean their pen or cage on a regular basis.

Coat Care

A guinea pig enjoys being lovingly and gently combed and brushed. Giving your pet that kind of attention is a way of showing affection in addition to keeping it clean and serving as a good skin massage. It also affords you the opportunity for early detection of vermin and skin diseases. Use the following guidelines for the various breeds of guinea pigs.

Short- or smooth-haired and Abyssinian guinea pigs need daily coat care only during shedding season. On the other hand, longhaired guinea pigs must be combed and brushed daily, because their hair can reach a length of 8 inches (20 cm) and more. From early on, accustom your guinea pig to being groomed even if its coat of hair is not yet fully developed.

Longhaired guinea pigs must be combed and brushed daily, or their hair will get matted.

Note: If you want to let your pet's hair grow really long, you have to roll it up on paper curlers.

Coat Care for Short Hair

Shorthaired and Abyssinian guinea pigs only need daily brushing when they are shedding, usually in spring and fall. Using a brush that is not too hard (see page 58, Drawing 1), give the coat a thorough going-over to remove the old hairs. If you brush your pet lovingly and gently, it will willingly submit to the procedure, even when it is not shedding season.

Coat Care for Long Hair

Daily grooming is a must for longhaired guinea pigs. Set the animal onto your lap with a warm cloth underneath it. Keep petting it and talk encouragingly to it and finally reward it with a treat.

Here's how to go about grooming your pet. First, disentangle with a broad-toothed comb. Spray the coat with mink oil beforehand until it's shiny. Sticky or matted areas, particularly on the hindquarters, should be cut out or washed with anti-tangle shampoo for cats (available in pet stores). Then blow dry your animal.

Bathing—Yes or No?

In general, there is no need to bathe your animal. Wash it only if it is extremely dirty—owing to diarrhea, for example—or for medical reasons such as a mite infestation, and then in lukewarm water, at 77 to 80.6°F (25–27°C). To combat vermin, use a special shampoo prescribed by the veterinarian; otherwise a very mild baby shampoo is sufficient.

If the claws are not clipped, they'll grow too long and interfere with the animal's walking.

1 Groom shorthaired coats daily only during the shedding season.

2 Bathing is necessary only when the hair is completely matted.

3 Cut the claws at a sharp downward angle.

4 Clean out dirty ears with a paper tissue.

Washing and Combing

If your pet's long hair is totally matted with sawdust, a bath is unavoidable (see Drawing 2). The best method: place a basin just large enough to hold the guinea pig in the sink. Fill the basin with lukewarm water and wash the guinea pig with a mild baby shampoo. Never submerge your pet's head. Rinse the shampoo out thoroughly and then dry the animal well with a heated towel; it must not be allowed to catch cold.

Finally, hold the guinea pig on your lap and comb its hair with the wide-toothed comb. Dry it with a blow-dryer or set it under an infrared light.

Note: It is essential to protect your pet against drafty air. Guinea pigs can catch cold very quickly, or even develop pneumonia.

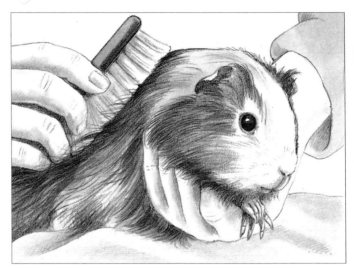

1 Shorthaired guinea pigs should only be groomed daily during their shedding season.

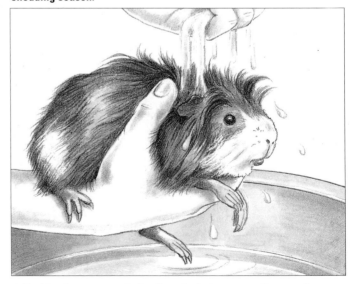

2 Bathing is necessary only when the hairs are totally matted.

3 Cutting should be done at a steep downward angle.

4 Clean out dirty ears with a tissue.

Overly Long Claws and Teeth

This problem rarely occurs in the wild. In a cage, however, the claws often grow faster than they can be worn down. Therefore, you must check the toes and claws regularly and clip the latter, if necessary.

Constant, continuing growth is also characteristic of guinea pig teeth. Give the animal plenty of hard food, including old bread and special types of pet treats for nibbling and gnawing (available in pet stores) so that the teeth can be worn down.

Cutting the Claws

In older guinea pigs, the claws often are no longer worn down in the natural way. Then they have to be trimmed regularly. Have an expert (a veterinarian or a breeder) show you the procedures first, since clipping the claws is not easy (see Drawing 3). You need to be aware of the following:

■ When clipping the claws, hold the guinea pig's paw gently and push the hair slightly to one side.

■ To keep the nail from splintering, you can use special clippers (available in pet stores). If you guide the tool correctly, however, standard nail clippers will also suffice.

■ Along with nerve endings, blood vessels—the quick—extend into the claws. If they are injured, the guinea pig will be in pain, and there will be blood. Make your cut just before the point where the "quick" begins, and angle it downward. Then the cut will conform to the shape of the claw.

■ To be on the safe side, don't cut very short. If bleeding does ensue, put disinfectant on a cotton pad and press it against the site of the injury.

■ In dark-clawed guinea pigs, the quick is difficult or impossible to see. It is best to have someone help you. One person can hold the guinea pig

and shine a flashlight on the claws from below, while the other does the clipping.

Cleaning the Eyes

Use a dampened, soft paper tissue to remove any crusts that form in the corners of your pet's eyes. Always wipe toward the nose.

A sudden, copious flow of tears is a sign of inflammation or injury. See the veterinarian about this.

Cleaning the Ears

The ears also need to be inspected regularly. Carefully remove any dust and dirt from the external part of the ear with a paper tissue. (See Drawing 4, page 59.) *Caution:* never use cotton swabs.

Dirty ears that have an unpleasant smell may be infested by ear mites. This condition can be recognized by the guinea pig's inclining his head on the side of the infested ear. See the veterinarian without delay (see page 76.)

Malocclusion

Unfortunately, malocculusion is often congenital in guinea pigs. The opposing incisors are positioned in such a way that they do not rub against one

The mother doesn't have to clean the young very much. They do that themselves just a few minutes after birth.

For two or three weeks the young ones stay close to their mother and are nursed by her during that period.

TIP

Longhair coats very quickly get matted with sawdust. The best thing to do is to use sawdust as a base for the bedding and put a thick layer of straw or hay on top of it. If snarls still appear, which frequently happens, cut the hair so that it doesn't touch the floor. If you want to let it grow very long, you have no choice but to roll up the hair in paper curlers.

another when the animal gnaws. As a result, they are not worn down and they grow unchecked. Regular cutting, which should be performed by the veterinarian, is necessary every two to three months.

The molars too, sometimes don't bite down correctly on each other. This may finally even keep the animal from eating. Unless you take it to the veterinarian immediately, it will starve to death.

A Clean Guinea Pig Home

If you keep a guinea pig, you have to ensure that it lives in clean, orderly surroundings.

Decaying straw, urine, feces, and rotting food remnants create an unappetizing, untidy mess where only bacteria and parasites thrive. In such a case, guinea pigs appear to really stink but it's not the poor animals' fault, since the blame clearly falls on their human owner. Regular, thorough cleaning of the cage and accessories is not something that can be neglected.

The water dispenser and food bowls must be cleaned every day:

■ Wash the dishes with boiling water. Do not use detergent.

61

■ Clean the gravity-flow water bottle with hot water also. Since it is hard to get a bottle brush into all the corners, use this trick: fill the bottle half full of water and stuff two or three sheets of paper toweling into it. By shaking the bottle you will create a pulp that will clean the bottle well. Finally, pour out the pulp and rinse out the bottle a few times.

■ Fill the gravity-flow water bottle with room-temperature water. Ice cold water causes digestive upsets in guinea pigs.

Clean the cage once a week:

■ Put the bedding in with other biodegradable materials. Kitty litter has to go into the garbage can.

Note: If you have a garden, you can toss the sawdust or straw onto your compost heap. Guinea pigs' feces decomposes quite well. Desiccated matter can even be placed directly on the flower beds. With larger quantities, ask a farmer or a riding stable whether they would accept the manure.

■ Scrub the bottom tray with hot water and an all-purpose cleanser.

Urinary calculus can best be dissolved with acetic acid or citric acid and removed

with a putty knife or a brush. Then rinse it out very thoroughly, so that the guinea pig's skin does not blister. Wipe the tray completely dry and add fresh bedding filler.

Rinse the top part of the cage in your bathtub with hot water once a month. Do so more frequently as needed.

Note: You need to disinfect the cage only once a year, as a preventive measure. Use a good mild nontoxic disinfectant, an all-purpose cleanser. If you have to disinfect because your pet is ill, ask your veterinarian for advice.

Guinea pigs clean their faces only with the inner edge of their hands, never with the whole palm.

Are Guinea Pigs Clever Animals?

You won't be able to teach them how to solve mathematical problems, which supposedly any idiot could do. To make up for that guinea pigs deal very gently with each other and they lend mutual assistance. I've heard the story of two guinea pigs who really worked together to escape from their outdoor enclosure. In a joint operation they pushed apart two boxes that barred the way out. One of them working alone certainly wouldn't have succeeded.

Tips for Coping with a Pregnant Guinea Pig

In the first four weeks, you will scarcely notice that your guinea pig is expecting (see page 83). If the female has mated without your knowledge, it will be difficult to be prepared for the coming event. That need not alarm you greatly, since basically a pregnant guinea pig needs no special treatment. Nonetheless, keep the following in mind:

■ Be very careful when you lift and carry the guinea pig. Alternatively, avoid carrying your pet around altogether.

■ Impress upon your children that they are not allowed to hug and cuddle with their pet during these weeks, but that they may pet it gently.

■ Give your pet plenty of green foods that are high in vitamins, or add vitamin supplements to its food.

■ Do not cancel the daily outing indoors or out in the yard, since even in the advanced stages of pregnancy guinea pigs still like to run around. The only thing they dislike is being chased—when you are trying to return them to their cage, for example.

■ Shortly before the due date, separate the sow from the boar, because he can mate with her as soon as 12 hours after the young are born. In addition, the boar's eagerness could distract the mother to such an extent that she would be unable to care for her young adequately (see Courting and Mating, page 82).

■ If you know from observation that the sex act has occurred, or if you believe (or even suspect) that mating has taken place unnoticed, it is a good idea to begin adding dry powdered milk to the guinea pig's food. This is primarily for the sake of the mother-to-be since her reserve of nutrients will be taxed as the gestation process gets underway.

■ If you haven't already done so, now is also the time to cut down on sunflower seeds, the most fattening of guinea pig foods.

Good Nutrition

Guinea pigs are not choosy about their food. They are undemanding and can quickly get used to certain foods. The only things they don't like are onions and potatoes.

The Staple: Hay

The "daily bread" of our guinea pigs is hay. If no fresh greens are available in winter, they can even live on hay and water exclusively. Hay consists of grass, clover, and wild herbs. The protein content of hay varies, depending on the components.

You can buy hay in relatively small bags in pet stores or supermarkets. If you need larger amounts, you can buy it inexpensively from a farmer.

Stinging nettle hay is the best choice and you can easily gather it yourself. Alfalfa hay is an excellent alternative; it is readily available in the better pet stores.

Things to Keep in Mind When You Buy

High-quality hay has an aromatic scent and is slightly greenish in color. *Rowen* (or aftermath) is hay from the second crop in a season. *Caution:* Old, yellowed, rotting, or moldy hay can be dangerous.

Green and Juicy Foods

These are the most natural and healthful foods for a guinea pig. Fodder plants, vegetables, and fruits are high in nutritional value and rich in protein, calcium, and vitamin C. The guinea pig is the only rodent that requires vitamin C.

Foods You Can Gather

The following, among others, are suitable for picking: field horsetail, dandelion, grass, coltsfoot, yarrow, ribwort, and alfalfa. Clover will cause a lot of flatulence. Therefore, serve only very little.

Note: Don't gather plants where there's a lot of traffic or where dogs are taken out. Pick only the plants you're sure you recognize.

From Kitchen and Garden

Apples, bananas, peanuts, kiwis, grapes, most varieties of lettuce (see page 68), carrots, peppers, parsley, and much more. Citrus and pitted fruits on account of their high vitamin C content, but just a little. Head salad has a high concentration of nitrates. Cabbage and pears cause flatulence. Potato sprouts and raw beans are poisonous.

Greens or lettuce can be planted in a bowl. Then the guinea pig will always have fresh, healthy food.

Commercial Feed Mixes

These contain grains, oat flakes, corn, peanuts, sunflower seeds, and pressed hay (pellets) with added vitamins and minerals. These mixes can serve as the only source of nourishment for 1 or 2 days.

One to two tablespoonfuls daily per guinea pig will be enough. Do not give your pet more than .4 to .7 ounces (10–20 g); otherwise, it will become overweight. If it is eating plenty of greens at the same time, you can reduce the amount of concentrated feedstuff.

Nibbles

Guinea pigs need plenty of foods to gnaw on to wear down their teeth (see page 59).

A large variety of nibbles can be found in pet shops. Hard bread without preservatives is good, provided it is not moldy or salted. Also suitable are young shoots and branches of birch, willow, or fruit trees (unsprayed!).

Drinking Water Is Important

Guinea pigs should always have water available. Tap water that has been allowed to stand and settle for a while is better than water straight from the faucet. Heavily chlorinated water should be boiled or bottled water should be served. Guinea pigs should not drink milk; it causes diarrhea.

Vitamins and Minerals

A salt lick provides your pet with the right salts in the proper ratio of components. However, not all guinea pigs like the salt lick. Hang it from the cage wire; if you leave it on the bottom of the cage, the stone will be softened by urine.

Vitamin preparations are available in pet stores. If your pet eats a healthy, varied diet high in vitamin C they are not absolutely necessary. In winter, a vitamin supplement is advisable, since fruits and vegetables are low in natural vitamins at this time of year.

The Right Way to Feed Your Pet

■ Feed your pet twice a day, always at the same time.
■ Never serve your pet too much at once.

Fruit should be well washed but not peeled, because most of the vitamins are found under the skin.

Hay is your guinea pig's "daily bread." Therefore a day's ration must always be on hand.

Anything that has not been eaten after one hour should be removed (except for hay).

■ Only fresh food is really good for the animal. Vegetables, etc., should not be shriveled, rotten, or moldy.

■ Hay and fresh greens should be available at all times. If you have no rack, fill a net with these foods and hang it in the cage; if left on the bottom of the cage, the food will be contaminated by feces and urine.

■ Fruits, cucumbers, and tomatoes need to be washed well, but not peeled, since most of the vitamins are under the peel. Remove the skin of peppers, however, since it is hard to chew. After washing, let vegetable drip dry.

■ Lettuce, especially head lettuce, needs to be washed because of the many harmful substances present. Dry it well, in a towel or in a salad spinner. Wet lettuce can be more harmful than unwashed lettuce.

■ Never serve your pet anything directly from the

67

refrigerator. Cold food could upset the guinea pig's stomach.
■ Twice a week, refill the gravity-flow water dispenser with water that has been allowed to stand for a while. If your pet doesn't know how to get at the water, gently push its nose against the drinking tube. It will get the idea.

Note: A guinea pig that drinks to excess is either sick or has not had any greens for quite a while. It also often drinks from boredom. If that is the cause, hang the bottle in the cage only at certain times of day.
■ Occasionally, give your pet something to gnaw on: willow or fruit tree branches or some old bread.
■ Guinea pigs like to be fed by hand; you can pet them while they eat from your hand.
■ Regular exercise is extremely important to keep your pet fit and healthy.

Diet for Overweight Guinea Pigs

If your pet is overweight, you need to put it on a diet. Fat animals become lazy and susceptible to disease.

Omit the extra treats. Serve your pet only 1.4–2.1 ounces (40–60 g) of juicy foods per day, and reduce the concentrate and grain feed to 0.7 ounces (20 g) per week. Give it only unsprayed branches to nibble and let it run around as much as possible.

Hay and straw can be given in unlimited quantities. Also, provide plenty of fresh water, supplemented with vitamin drops, if possible.

Note: If your pet is extremely overweight, seek your veterinarian's advice.

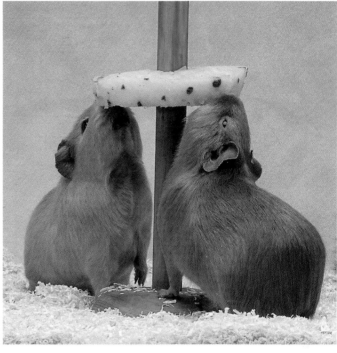

This inventive way to suspend food will provide variety in the cage and also keep the guinea pig fit.

See the table to the right. When you put together the animal's food, strive for a well-balanced mix. The presented tips are suggestions. Experiment with what your animal likes best.

Food Plan

	Food and Quantity	
Day and Time	**Morning**	**Afternoon/Early Evening**
Monday	0.7 ounce (20 g) commercial mix (1–2 tablespoons), 1 or 2 lettuce leaves, 1 small carrot, 1 apple quarter	1 rack full of fresh grasses and clover and alfalfa hay
Tuesday	0.7 ounce (20 g) commercial mix, 1 or 2 lettuce leaves, 1 thick slice of cucumber, 1 kiwi quarter	1 rack full of dandelion leaves or kale and cabbage
Wednesday	0.7 ounce (20 g) commercial mix, 1 or 2 lettuce leaves, 2 broccoli rosettes, 1 apple quarter	1 rack full of young stinging nettles and/or alfalfa hay
Thursday	0.7 ounce (20 g) commercial mix, 1 or 2 lettuce leaves, 1 slice of pepper, 1 tomato quarter, 1 orange section	1 rack full of fresh grasses and clover, celery tops, cauliflower, or dandelion
Friday	0.7 ounce (20 g) commercial mix, 1 or 2 lettuce leaves, 1 piece of red beet, 1 apple quarter	1 rack full of fresh grasses and herbs, broccoli, turnips, and kale
Saturday	0.7 ounce (20 g) commercial mix, 1 or 2 stalks of parsley, 1 thick slice of zucchini, 1 slice of melon	1 rack full of field horsetail, coltsfoot, and other plants
Sunday	0.7 ounce (20 g) commercial mix, 1 or 2 lettuce leaves, 1 cabbage leaf, half a carrot, 1 cucumber slice	1 rack full of grasses and wild herbs
Daily	Put the amount of hay the guinea pig can eat in one day in the rack	
Once a week	0.5 ounce (15 g) of old, rock-hard bread or a nibble stick, 1 fruit tree branch, and—in fall—dry leaves	

Preventive Care and Health Problems

By nature, guinea pigs are robust animals. If they are properly cared for and fed and have plenty of exercise in addition, then you are taking the best possible steps to prevent illness.

The Right Diet for Good Health

Because of their special digestive system, guinea pigs need to eat foods that are high in fiber. Their diet must include a great number of plants and herbs (see page 64), which have to be made available all year round.

Dirty surroundings easily give rise to diseases that can infect the guinea pig, other pets, and human beings too. It is therefore essential for your pet's well being that you regularly clean the cage, accessories, and food dishes. Wash your hands after caring for and touching your guinea pig and teach your child to do the same. As a rule, no animal should be kissed or pressed against bare human skin.

Health Problems for Humans

If a tendency to allergies is present, this tendency can become sensitized when com-ing into contact with guinea pigs. If any allergic reactions occur (itching, reddening of the skin) consult an allergist at once.

Zoonoses: Diseases that are transmissible from animals to humans occur infrequently in guinea pigs, with the exception of skin diseases. If there is any question go to the veterinarian and consult your doctor.

Fungal diseases: The symptoms of microsporosis and trichophytosis (tinea) in both animals and humans are characteristic, frequently circular red patches on the skin accompanied by severe itching and hair loss. Then the guinea pig has to go to the veterinarian, and the human to a dermatologist.

Mange mites: These occur relatively frequently in guinea pigs because of poor living conditions. They can be transmitted to humans through direct skin contact, causing pustular eruptions accompanied by itching.

Salmonellosis: Salmonella infections are relatively common in guinea pigs. The infection can be transferred to humans, especially children.

Guinea pigs prefer to live in communities. Keeping them individually could make them sick.

Because of their particular digestive system, guinea pigs require a vegetarian diet rich in fiber.

Lymphocytic choriomeningitis (LCM): Up to now, guinea pigs have not been shown to be carriers of this disease.

The First Symptoms of Illness

If you pay attention to your guinea pig on a regular basis, you will immediately be aware of any change in its behavior and appearance.

If the guinea pig no longer squeals excitedly when you bring it food, but crouches listlessly in a corner with sunken, dull eyes and an arched back, then something is the matter. If its coat is rough and dull and the animal is shedding more than usual, scratching itself continuously, panting, or displaying other unusual behaviors, these are the first signs of a possible illness. You need to keep in mind that the small rodents have little ability to express their feelings through facial expressions, and disease states are difficult to detect early. Concealing illness is a part of their survival strategy in their natural habitat, to keep from being immediately excluded

TIP

You can help a weak animal by giving it green feed with herbs, vitamins, oat flakes, and wheat germ and by having the veterinarian give it an injection to build it up. Fresh air will do it good. By no means must the animal catch cold, however, and it should not be used for breeding.

from the pack. It is entirely possible that your guinea pig may have been ill for quite some time and in need of a veterinarian's speedy assistance. If you have doubts about your pet's health, always go to the veterinarian at once.

Minor Health Problems

If you take action quickly, relatively minor health problems will often be resolved. Here are some things you can do to help your pet yourself:

Mild diarrhea: The signs are a smeary stool that is not well-formed and is light in color. The overall health of the animal remains good. First, replace juicy foods and greens with hay, and give your pet lukewarm chamomile tea or fennel tea to drink. Feed it willow branches and grated carrots. Make sure the bedding is dry, and add a bottom layer of filler (oat straw or hay) for extra warmth. See the veterinarian if the stool is not firm again after two days.

Mild constipation: Check to see whether the perineal cavity around the anus is congested with feces. If it is, empty it by pressing it carefully, using a dampened cotton swab. If your pet's stool consists of tiny, hard pellets, first check the water bottle to see whether it is working properly. A lack of water is frequently the cause! Discontinue grain feed for a few days, give your pet cucumber and melon to eat, and use a disposable syringe (minus the needle) to squirt one tablespoonful of natural sauerkraut juice three times a day into the guinea pig's cheek pouch on one side. Moving your fingers in a circle, massage the animal's abdomen repeatedly. Stinging nettle hay, sorrel, and dandelion leaves also will help. If no improvement is evident after 24 hours, consult the veterinarian.

Runny nose caused by irritation: Eliminate possible causes, such as dusty hay or caustic cleaning products that produce gases.

If a guinea pig is constipated it should not be given grain foods for a few days.

Checklist for Health Problems and Diseases

What You Notice	Possible Causes You Can Remedy Yourself
Guinea pig sits around listlessly, does not greet you	Boredom, lack of a social partner, too little attention, wrong items in the cage, no outings for exercise
Does not eat	Unsuitable or spoiled food, lack of water, ambient temperature too low or too high, drafty air, wet bedding
Drooling, coat sticky in lower jaw area	Inadequate abrasion of teeth—give foods to gnaw as a preventive (see page 66)
Diarrhea	Sudden change in diet (from dry feed to greens), food spoiled or too cold, water stagnant or too cold, living conditions too cool or too damp, drafty air
Straining without passage of stool and urine	Lack of exercise, defective water bottle, sudden switch from greens to dry feed exclusively
Sneezing, coughing	Drafty air, irritation due to bedding (desiccated matter, for example), caustic cleaning products, hay that is dusty or has gone bad
Tearing eyes, reddened or possibly swollen lids, watery to purulent discharge	Irritation due to dust or foreign bodies, injury caused by scratch, hair that juts into the narrow crack between the eyelids (longhaired or Abyssinian guinea pigs)
Accelerated breathing	Overheating, anxiety, stress
Increased scratching	Unclean living conditions, poor coat care (mats)
Limping	Overly long claws, wrong bedding (cat litter, for example)
Slight bleeding	Superficial skin injuries
Bare patches in coat	Vitamin deficiency due to nutritional imbalance, biting coat because there is inadequate roughage

Dangerous Accompanying Symptoms	Possible Diagnosis Needing Prompt Treatment by Veterinarian
Apathy, lack of appetite, diarrhea, emaciation, coat stands on end	Serious digestive problem or infectious causes
Foul-smelling diarrhea, sometimes tinged with blood, hunched back, apathy, sticky nostrils	Poisoning, intestinal infection (salmonellosis, coccidiosis); bring along stool sample, isolate animal
Reddened skin, hair loss, crusty discharge around the mouth, refusal to eat	Tooth defects, injuries to mucous membranes of mouth, vitamin C deficiency, viral infection
Failure to eat, increasing weakness, sunken eyes, apathy, wasting, emaciation	Dysbacteria, intestinal coccidiosis, food poisoning, inflammation of the bowels, desiccation
Elevated temperature, dragging hind legs, convulsions, difficulty in breathing	Constipation, urinary problem, urinary tract infection, guinea pig lameness
Apathy, difficulty in breathing, nasal discharge, weight loss	Contagious cold, bronchitis, bronchial pneumonia (infectious diseases)—isolate animal from others at once
Aversion to light, reddening of conjunctiva, clouding of cornea, bulging eyes	Conjunctivitis, corneal ulcer, glaucoma
Puffing out of cheeks, heaving sides, blue coloration of mucous membranes	Heatstroke, shock; see veterinarian immediately
Sticky hair, smeary or crusty patches, scratching accompanied by convulsions, head held at an angle	Guinea pig mange, skin fungus infection, inflammation of auditory canal
Reluctance to move, reluctance to place weight on one extremity, dragging of hind legs, lack of balance	Inflammation of balls of feet, strained muscle, broken bone, spinal column injury, skull trauma, inflammation in inner ear
Convulsions, self-injury through biting	Guinea pig mange
Circular bare patches, symmetrical hair loss on both sides	Nutritional deficiency diseases, mycoses, hormonal disorder

The Sick Guinea Pig

Guinea pigs are unable to express pain through gesture, facial expression, or speech. Their behavior, therefore, provides few clues to the severity of a disease. Do not put off the trip to the veterinarian for too long.

The Visit to the Veterinarian

It is best to transport your guinea pig to the doctor's office in a tightly latched basket or a pet carrier (see Drawing 1).

To assist the veterinarian in making a diagnosis, it is helpful to have the following information:

Where does the animal come from? How long has it been in your possession? How old is it? What changes have you noticed in its behavior, and when did they first become apparent? What do you feed your pet? Have you changed its diet recently? Is there any change in its stool or urine (ideally, bring along samples)? What is its environment (cage, cage location, items in cage like bedding and toys, opportunity for exercise outside cage, etc.) like? Has the guinea pig had contact with other pets?

1 The sick animal will feel safe in this carrier.

2 It is best to apply ointment with a cotton swab.

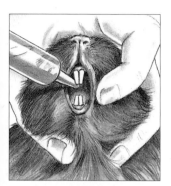

3 Let the water drip in slowly.

4 Dab the corners of the eyes.

5 Clean excrement from the anus.

Tips on Care

Housing: If possible, separate the animal from other guinea pigs by putting it in a cage alone as a precaution. If the disease is contagious, change the bedding frequently. Disinfect the cage and accessories.

Location: A draft-free, quiet, room not in direct sunlight and with a comfortable temperature.

Liquids: The sick animal absolutely has to maintain its fluid intake, or it will dehydrate. Using a disposable syringe (without a needle), slowly drip water or tea into one of the cheek pouches. Repeatedly interrupt the process to let your pet masticate (see Drawing 3).

Applying ointment: With minor injuries, carefully cut away the coat around the circumference of the wound. Clean the site and rub on a suitable ointment until absorbed (see Drawing 2).

Treating eyes: If your pet has swollen conjunctiva, carefully dab warm water at the corners of the eyes (see Drawing 4). Reduce the amount of light in the room while your pet is ill.

Maintaining cleanliness: In case of diarrhea, wipe matted hairs with a damp cloth.

Putting Your Pet to Sleep

If your guinea pig is suffering from a painful and incurable disease, having it put to sleep is sometimes unavoidable. In making the decision be sure to keep in mind that what every animal wants, above all, is to live. In older guinea pigs, diseases and disabilities (poor hearing and dim eyesight) develop only gradually, and with time the animal gets used to this condition. It does not necessarily suffer great pain.

In consultation with the veterinarian, decide whether your guinea pig really needs to be put to sleep.

Children are often unwilling to see that the time has come to say farewell to a beloved playmate. It is up to you to explain the concept of death in an appropriate way.

The death of an animal, even a natural death, is always painful. After all, we are losing a friend, a family member, who has become very dear to us. Sometimes a "surviving" guinea pig too, grieves and cannot deal with the loss of a partner. Giving the animal a new partner is often a good solution. But take care in getting them used to each other (see page 101).

Planned Breeding of Guinea Pigs

Guinea pigs have no difficulty at all in presenting their owner with progeny. Breeding purebred guinea pigs will reward animal fanciers with a great deal of pleasure and diversion, but it mean plenty of work as well.

Breeding Purebred Guinea Pigs

If you want to start a breeding program, you need a very good grasp of genetics. A good breeder's goal, after all, is to produce animals that are not only healthy but beautiful as well. With a guinea pig, "beautiful" means that the animal conforms as closely as possible to the guidelines set forth for the various breeds in a breed standard (see page 32). A breeder's primary aim is to exhibit his or her animals at shows and have them judged. To that end, a breeder maintains a studbook and specializes in very specific features of hair and color.

Choosing the Parents

Both parents have to be healthy and vigorous and of the right age.

Sows cannot be used for breeding until they are four to six months old. Pregnancy too

early in life is harmful to them. Frequently they die while giving birth or have stillborn young. Sometimes the first litter has to be delivered by cesarean section. Such females are more susceptible to disease later on, suffer from growth disturbances, and have a diminished life expectancy. However, a female should be no older than one year at the time of her first litter; otherwise, she may fail to conceive or often gives birth to premature or stillborn young. Females can continue to be bred until they are four to five years old.

Boars can be used for breeding once they are six to seven months old. At the age of six years, they should be removed from your breeding program. Usually nature will determine how long a male can be used for breeding. He is not forced to mate and is subjected to less physical stress than a brood sow. As for the rest, the age of the male has no influence on the state of health of the offspring. If there are hereditary malformations—malocclusions, for example, which often become apparent only when the animal is two or three years

A guinea pig mother has only two teats; but the young ones don't fight over the source of milk.

old—the male should be removed from the breeding program immediately.

Inbreeding

Inbreeding—breeding of closely related individuals—is used in guinea pig breeding. A mother is mated with the best-developed son, a father with the most ideal daughter. The purpose is to breed for characteristics such as size, color, and hair length, as well as body frame, constitution, stability, and longevity. With animals that have the same characteristics—from the same family, say—a particular breeding goal

can be quickly achieved. Of course, undesirable characteristics often are passed on as well. Generally speaking, you need to keep the following in mind:

■ Do not breed siblings with one another.

■ Mating half brothers and half sisters is possible if the parents exhibit no signs of hereditary defects such as malformations or susceptibility to disease. To rule out hidden defects through inbreeding, it is better to cross only half brothers and sisters whose parents and grandparents were bred by you or whose family

The female is ready for mating every 14–18 days. Before that, the male must keep up a constant courtship.

Giving birth is entirely without problems. As soon as one pup is licked clean, the next one appears.

tree is ascertainable. With guinea pigs from a pet store, that usually is not possible, and therefore the risk is too great.

■ Inbreeding should continue for no more than two generations. Otherwise, there is a risk of malformations, such as missing eyes, crippled feet, damage to internal organs, and diminished life expectancy.

■ Be sure to continue to incorporate an unrelated individual with the same characteristics and desirable features in your breeding program.

Note: To breed for certain hair and color features, you need to know their genetic

formula and to be well informed about the laws of genetics. Discussing this topic in greater detail exceeds the scope of this book.

Life as a Couple

If you want to give your female a male as a companion, you need to get the two used to each other first. Don't simply place the new guinea pig in the cage with your already established pet; that can have bad consequences. If the cage is large enough (at least 32 × 32 × 18 inches, or 80 × 80 × 45 cm), you can divide it down the middle with a sliding wire partition. Otherwise, leave the two guinea pigs in their cages and place them side by side. In this way, the couple-to-be can see and sniff one another. After one or two days, remove the partition or put the two guinea pigs into the same cage, under your supervision. At first they will try to command each other's respect and to nudge each other lightly. That is part of the ritual. Only if they bite each other do you have to separate them and try again later. If they still do not get along, you have no other choice than to try again with a different partner.

81

Note: Rub perfume on your hands and pet the guinea pigs at length. That will mask the animals' own scent for a time—that is, they will smell the same—and it will have a calming effect. By the time their own scent reasserts itself, they will have become so used to each other that no more conflicts will develop.

As a rule, males and females live together in great harmony. The male will deal amicably with the female. Should differences of opinion ever occur, the boar usually gives in. If he becomes too pushy, the sow will give him a light nip on the nose or even pull out a few of the hairs on the back of his neck. The male will not only endure everything patiently, but also let the female have especially tasty morsels of food, over which two females or two males often would fight stubbornly.

Courtship and Mating

Actually guinea pigs are in heat all year long. All that is needed is assiduous courtship—which the male will provide with great persistence.

The boar circles around the sow many times, with leisurely movements and swaying

hindquarters, making sputtering noises. He then tries to brush his flank against the female's body. She resists vigorously by sitting up on her hind legs, stretching her front legs straight out, and opening her mouth wide to show her teeth. That looks far more dangerous than it is. Every 14 to 18 days the sow is in heat—that is, sexually receptive. The eggs that have developed in her ovaries are in a stage favorable to fertilization. Now the suitor finds acceptance. The female lies down on her belly and lifts her hindquarters in the air.

Little guinea pigs come into the world fully developed and begin to groom themselves right away.

The act of mating lasts only a few seconds. Afterward the two guinea pigs groom each other conspicuously and thoroughly, paying special attention to the genital area.

Pregnancy

If the female has conceived—that is, if the eggs have been fertilized and attached themselves in the uterus, the young guinea pigs will be born an average of 68 days later. At first you will have no indication that the sow is pregnant, since no change in her behavior is apparent. The male is very attentive during this time and lets the mother-to-be have the best place at the food bowl.

Not until the fourth week does the female become more rounded in shape, with enlarged teats.

In the last two weeks of the gestation period, she is decidedly plump; the young now account for over half of her body weight. You can clearly see and feel them move inside their mother's body.

The expectant mother makes no special preparations for the impending birth. She makes no attempt to build a nest. Consequently, it is often difficult for an inexperienced guinea pig owner to know what is in store.

Should the Male Be Present During the Birth?

With guinea pigs, there is no danger that the father will behave aggressively toward the young or, even worse, bite them to death. Don't worry about leaving him in the cage. Usually the sow doesn't care whether the boar is present or not. Sometimes, however, he even can have a calming effect on the expectant mother. There have been cases in which the father helped lick the newborns dry. In general, the birth process seems to be a matter of indifference to him, since he usually stays at the other end of the cage, eats, or grooms himself, thereby expressing his lack of interest.

Guinea pigs like to slip into a little house and snuggle up against each other there.

Birth

Like everything else with guinea pigs, giving birth generally is no problem at all. Since the young usually are born at night, at dawn, or at dusk, you often will be taken by surprise. Certain signs, including digging in the bedding, swollen genitals, discharge of mucus, or visible contractions of the abdomen may indicate that the event is imminent.

The birth process: The female stays in a sitting position and expels the young guinea pig—or pup—under her body. She reaches between her front legs to tear open the fetal membrane, then eats it. That is important; otherwise, the newborn would very quickly suffocate. Then the mother licks its mouth, nose, and eyes clean. Scarcely is one little pup taken care of before the next one announces itself. Usually some blood is expelled at the conclusion of the process, along with the afterbirth (placenta), all or part of which the mother consumes.

Nose to nose. That's how the tiny little guinea pig establishes early contact with its mother.

Newborn and Already Independent

The unusual thing about guinea pigs is that they are completely developed when they come into the world. Their eyes are open—they opened two weeks before, inside their mother's body— and their coat is thick, glossy, and silky as soon as their mother licks it clean.

Little guinea pigs are nidifugous; that is, they are able to walk right away and even to eat grass, hay, and other solid foods. Even their milk teeth are replaced by their permanent set, while the young are still inside their mother's body. As soon as one or two hours after birth, young guinea pigs already begin to bustle about in their cage quite cheerfully, though they stay near their mother at all times. They are nursed by her for two to three weeks, but they already are eating fodder and hay as well. This makes raising orphaned guinea pig babies fairly easy.

If the young become orphans, it is best to give them to a guinea pig that has just given birth herself. If the opportunity does not present itself, milk for rearing kittens (available at pet stores) has proven useful. Give it to the little guinea pig with a disposable syringe (without a needle), feeding the animal slowly, drop by drop. During the first two weeks, feed the little animals approximately every one to two hours, 1 to 1.5 milliliters at a time. In the third week, increase the amount to 2 milliliters. Nighttime feedings are not necessary.

Note: Put the pups with an adult guinea pig, either a female that has already borne young or a neutered male. The pups will learn what they can eat from the mature animal's example. Make sure the male or the older female is nice to the young guinea pigs and does not deliberately annoy them.

How Often May the Female Be Bred?

As we have already said, a female guinea pig is ready to mate again immediately after giving birth. Letting nature take its course is best for large-scale breeders only, whose goal is to obtain large numbers of pups. Let the mother have breaks between her pregnancies. You are in the best position to know whether she was weakened by bearing the

T I P

Move the male out of the cage he and the female share before the litter is born. The problem is that the female will come into estrus again a few hours after giving birth and allow the male to mate with her. Then offspring can be expected again about two months later. You can let the male return to his family only after about three to four days.

last litter. Let her have time to recover. Don't breed her again until her young are about five or six weeks old—that is, ready to go to new homes. Having her bred once or twice a year is a good average, and that will not be too great a strain on her.

Note: The intervals between the pregnancies should not exceed 6 to 12 months. Otherwise, the sow might fail to conceive or might refuse to let the boar near her.

Development of the Young

Weight: At birth the pups weigh 2.5 to 4 ounces (71–113 g). For the first few days their weight remains stable and sometimes they even lose weight. But then, up to the age of five or six weeks, they start putting on 3–4 g daily. Weigh them from time to time, so you can be sure they're thriving.

Behavior: It is delightful to see how active the little animals are shortly after birth. They scarcely glimpse the light of day before they begin to groom themselves to perfection. Consequently you will seldom see their mother licking them clean. The very same day they have a real hopping fit; they jump straight up into the air, with all four feet off the ground, and double back while still in the air. They chase each other, scoot into the little house and out again, and clear obstacles with ease.

Food: The mother will feed her pups regularly. She has only two teats, but the little guinea pigs do not fight over the milk source. Each one waits calmly until its turn comes. Besides sow's milk, they will consume hay, lettuce, dandelions, oat flakes, and commercial guinea pig feed.

Note: The soft excrements from their mother's appendix are vitally important for them, because they contain vitamins B and K.

Interaction: Generally, the family gets along fine. The young obey their father as well as their mother. They do everything jointly. They eat together, groom themselves, snuggle up together, and apparently have a lot to say to one another. When out of their cage they troop along in single file, even inside your home. If a little one goes astray the mother or father will respond to its forlorn squeals at once, guiding it back to the others.

Sexual maturity: The females are sexually mature at

What Are Nidifugous Animals?

The guinea pig is a nidifugous (nest fleeing) animal. Granted, the word sounds a little odd, because fear is also an element in fleeing. But the guinea pigs aren't afraid at all. The name nidifugous is given to animals who can get up on their legs right after birth and begin walking. That means they don't stay crouching in the nest. On the other hand, little birds, cats, dogs, and human babies first have to learn to walk. These life forms are called nidicolous animals.

Little guinea pigs are able to walk right after birth and can even eat grass, hay, and other solid food.

the age of five weeks. If you want to keep the young, which at this time are ready to go to new homes, you have to separate them from their parents and keep the males and females in separate cages as well. The males do not reach sexual maturity until they are nine to ten weeks old. You may leave them all together until that time, but then separation is essential. Otherwise, dominance fights will inevitably break out (see page 91).

Understanding Your Pet and Keeping It Busy

No guinea pig is like any other. Each one has its own peculiarities, which are clearly apparent the very first time you approach your new pet. One guinea pig will eat out of your hand the first day, while another needs more time before it is ready to do that. Get to know your pet; then you will know exactly how to deal with it.

Winning your pet's confidence is the first step to hand taming.

Becoming Familiar with Behavior Problems

Have you ever listened attentively to your little housemate? To understand your pet, you need to know what it is trying to tell you with its various sounds and movements.

Anatomical Characteristics

The guinea pig's scientific name is *Cavia aperea porcellus*, which means roughly "the little pig that lives in the cave." A certain resemblance to pigs is undeniable, though the two species are unrelated. Once again, here is a summary of the major anatomical features.

Bone structure: Guinea pigs have very delicate bones that are easily bruised and broken if they fall. Avoid squeezing and hugging them too tightly (see page 21).

Feet: They are bare; that is, the hair extends only to the foot joint. The front feet have four toes and claws each; the hind feet have three toes and claws apiece. Unlike most other rodents, guinea pigs never hold their food firmly in both front feet though they

Sometimes guinea pigs will lift off the ground to get at tasty food.

sometimes place one foot on it. They clean their face only with the inner edge of their front feet, never with the entire surface of the paw. They stand on the entire sole of the foot, but walk only on their toes—a walk that resembles swift running.

Claws: Because their claws are rather wide, guinea pigs are also described as "hoof-pawed."

Adapted for Survival

Guinea pigs are not considered exactly intelligent, but they are highly social. There are reasons for that. The wild forebears of the domestic guinea pig specialized in eating grasses. Because the food all but grew right into their mouths, they had no need to develop great intellectual abilities in order to survive. Instead, they developed patterns of social behavior that enabled them to live peaceably in their community, since banding together in a pack offered them the greatest possible protection.

Most wild cavies' traits are based on the fact that rather than fighting their enemies they flee to safety. The abilities and behavior patterns were not lost in the course of their domestication.

Fighting Over Rank Order

Generally, a guinea pig pack consists of one boar and five or six sows. There is no room for a second boar. Only a male who has proved himself to be the strongest in the struggle for dominance will rule over his harem in the role of "pasha." All other males are forbidden to mate with a female. When males are young, they form small groups at the edge of the clan and keep to themselves. But when puberty begins, this unity ceases; they start to fight over the females.

Don't buy a food dish that's too big because the animal might sit in it.

First they try to impress one another. They stretch their legs to full length in order to appear taller; emit a hissing snarl and make chattering noises with their teeth; and slowly move in circles around each other. Each tries to take a nip out of the other's flank. Finally, they leap at one another and bite each other's neck or chest. This stage can last up to five minutes, and it will be repeated until one of the two males is defeated. The loser has to leave the pack and stand his ground elsewhere.

Note: He will have a miserable existence in an enclosure. The defeated boar is mercilessly driven away from the feeding place; finds nowhere to sleep, and is forced to waste away. Don't hesitate too long; put the guinea pig in his own enclosure, far away from the victor.

The Role of the Females

Generally, sows get along very well, but they have a hierarchy as well. There is a lead female who maintains order among her group and among the young. Often she displays a specific behavior: sitting on her hind legs, she slowly wiggles her hindquarters back and forth, chattering her teeth all the while. Occasionally, the

Whoever proves to be the stronger male will rule over the harem as a "pasha."

Can Guinea Pigs Get Nasty?

As a rule, guinea pigs are peaceful animals. Nevertheless, males can become enemies when they're contending for a female. Then they open their mouths wide and bare their long gnawing teeth. That's how they threaten each other. As a result some nipping may take place, if one of the two doesn't voluntarily retreat.

If two males, however, have *never* been exposed to a female, it is possible for them to live together peacefully (see p. 16).

Females don't fight with each other. If males become annoying, females flash their teeth at them threateningly.

lead male has to intervene if a subordinate female becomes too unruly.

The females also concern themselves with the well-being and progress of the young. While they are still small, young guinea pigs graze with the females in little groups. They nurse from their own mothers as well as other lactating females. Beginning in the second week of life, the young associate more and more with the dominant male (alpha), who helps wean them from their mothers. Nursing stops as of the third week on.

Note: If you keep a guinea pig clan in an enclosure, you have to make sure that the young males go to new homes as soon as they reach sexual maturity, if not earlier—that is, at nine to ten weeks of age. This is necessary to prevent fighting and the proliferation of unplanned offspring.

Survival Strategy

Guinea pigs have abilities that enable them to survive despite their numerous enemies, which include snakes, foxes, and birds of prey. Their familiarity with the complex network of well-beaten trails that link their hiding places

and feeding grounds, allow them to make a quick escape. They move swiftly and nimbly through the tallest grass to make them less likely to be discovered by enemies. They maintain close contact with one another at all times on their paths. They trot along in single file, one behind another, keeping the young ones between them. They communicate by means of gurgling or chuckling sounds, which never quite cease. One of the animals stands guard while the group grazes. As soon as it hears even the slightest noise, it gives a loud squeal, whereupon all the guinea pigs vanish in a flash. If a guinea pig gets really stuck, it throws itself down on its back and plays dead. Sometimes the enemy is deceived by this ploy. Because guinea pigs reproduce in such great numbers, nature has ensured that they cannot be wiped out.

Guinea Pig Language

Anyone who wants to understand the language of guinea pigs has to both watch and listen well, since the animals' vocalizations are often combined with certain body language (see page 96).

93

Squealing: It sounds like the whistling of a tea kettle, signifies a quite unmistakable plea for food, and is the only vocalization that the guinea pig reserves exclusively for communication with humans.

Whimpering or pitiful squealing: It is produced by a young guinea pig that has lost its way, cannot see its mother or siblings at the moment, or is frightened by some noise. A guinea pig kept alone will also whimper to solicit contact. If that happens, we need to pay attention to our little charge.

Clucking and cooing: Making soothing cooing sounds, the mother runs to her young. Gently clucking, she promises them protection and warmth. In fact her clucking is a sound that generally expresses contentment all around. It may be given further emphasis with leaps and bounds.

Grunting: This is the friendliest kind of greeting among guinea pigs. Members of a clan grunt when they meet each other outdoors. Then they engage in mutual sniffing, including nose contact.

Snarling and chattering: A guinea pig that snarls feels weak. It may also snarl at a human. Usually it also drops its head, a sign that it means peace. If the gesture is not understood, the fear-inspired snarling intensifies to an enraged chattering of teeth, the only threatening gesture guinea pigs know. This sharpening of the teeth is a prelude to combat between rivals, and usually the matter rests there. Leave your pet alone if it trembles threateningly or you may get a sharp bite.

Growling and sputtering: The male makes these sounds when he courts a female in heat.

Chirping: Domestic guinea pigs make these sounds very seldom, if ever. These very high-pitched squealing tones are uttered with great intensity. When this "song" is heard, all the other guinea pigs in the vicinity freeze in their tracks. It may be a behavior meant to substitute for another behavior.

A lively reaction to a familiar, loving voice.

Regular and thorough body grooming are part of a healthy guinea pig's behavior pattern.

Sensory Capacities

Because guinea pigs take flight rather than fight, they have to be equipped with excellent sensory organs in order to detect danger promptly.

Hearing: Guinea pigs hear extremely well. They are able to distinguish clear tones, in particular, in a range up to 33 kHz, while humans hear them only up to 20 kHz. The cochlea of their inner ear has four spirals (humans have only two-and-a-half); thus there is room for more auditory cells.

Vision: Their vision is also quite well developed. Their field of vision is relatively broad, which allows them to see enemies early, from all sides, without having to move their head. Experiments show that guinea pigs can also distinguish colors (see page 108).

Smell: Their sense of smell, which is 1,000 times better than a human's, plays a role primarily in sexual and social behavior. An animal that is not part of the clan is detected by its smell, and the various members of a guinea pig's human family are also perceived by their scent. The guinea pig's marking of both its partner and its territory with urine plays an important role.

Taste: We will not go further into the question of whether guinea pigs distinguish sweet from sour and for this reason prefer a strawberry to an orange. In any event, they have their taste preferences. A little imitation probably plays a role also; what the adult guinea pigs like can't be bad.

Touch: The tactile hairs that grow around the muzzle help the guinea pig to get its bearings (even in the dark) and guide it around obstacles. The animal also measures the width of openings with these sensitive feelers, thus making sure that it will not get stuck if it wants to squeeze its way through.

Body Language

To understand your guinea pig, you have to be familiar with its body language. The more you know about it, the more accurately you will be able to read your pet's behavior.

When danger threatens, the sleeping house is a good place to hide.

It's also nice to climb up on and have a little snack.

Guinea pigs also need a place in the cage in which they can feel safe on all sides.

Sniffing at one another: In order to recognize each other guinea pigs touch noses to make scent contact. Alternatively, they may smell the anal area. They are checking to see whether the guinea pig is a stranger to the pack and to determine its gender. If it is a female, they want to know whether she is willing to mate.

Trying to impress: Males try to look "big" by stretching their legs to full length and drawing themselves up to full height.

Alertness: If it feels uneasy about something, it stretches its head out attentively, presses itself to the ground, and tries to use all its senses to understand whether there is any danger.

Fearful: When a guinea pig is afraid, it will do one of two things. If it fears being attacked by another animal, it may lay on its back and play dead. Alternatively, if your pet feels helpless and in need of protection, it presses itself against the wall of its cage and draws its legs in.

A sign of strength: A guinea pig will lift its head at right angles as a sign of strength.

Warning: A female will warn a male to stay away from her by showing her teeth with her mouth wide open.

Begging for food: If, when you approach the cage, your guinea pig stands on its hind legs, it is most likely hoping that you will be giving it food.

Relaxing: When completely relaxing and enjoying the comforts of home, a guinea pig stretches.

High spirits: When your pet is in a good mood, you'll notice that it will leap around to express this feeling.

Getting the Guinea Pig Settled Properly

No pet is more perfect for children than a guinea pig. It loves to be petted and cuddled, and the more you play with it, the livelier and brighter it will be.

The New Home

Bring your new guinea pig home by the shortest possible route.

At home, set the little travel carrier in the cage, open it, and wait for the guinea pig to come out on its own. In the cage, there should be a thick layer of hay or straw on top of the bedding, lukewarm water in the gravity-flow water dispenser, a small helping of mixed grains in the food bowl, one apple quarter, and one leaf of lettuce.

The guinea pig can conceal itself in the hay; from this safe hiding place, it can observe everything in peace and quiet.

Feeling at Home

It is a good idea to set the cage on a table so that the guinea pig can see that there's nothing threatening in its environment. Otherwise, if you keep it on the floor, the animal will see only its owner's feet. It will sit there quietly for a while and maybe nibble at straw or hay.

It is over the initial shock when it starts to eat and drink, possibly even washing itself afterward. Now you can begin the process of hand-taming it, petting it, and talking to it. You need to let it run around out of the cage, so that it also can get to know the room in which it will live from now on.

Put a few treats here and there for the guinea pig to find and it will soon feel comfortable in its new surroundings.

Guinea Pigs and Children: Making Friends

Your child has been looking forward to his or her new playmate, but right now the relationship isn't working quite the way it was supposed to. You must now step in so that your child will understand that everything takes time. No doubt the guinea pig will enjoy being petted. But first of all it has to get used to a great many new things.

Be consistent and firm, and teach your child to share the responsibilities of feeding, cage-cleaning, grooming, and other little chores. That's the only way your child will learn that love for a living creature also means being patient.

TIP
▼

A shy and fearful guinea pig needs a long time before it will gain confidence in you. Pet it a lot and whenever possible feed it by hand. Instead of the little sleeping house give it plenty of straw in its cage, so that the animal can't become a recluse. You must exercise patience.

A marvelous guinea pig pyramid.
Even when it comes to eating,
guinea pigs stick close together.

Hand-taming Your Pet

Since guinea pigs have been in human care such a long time, our presence and our smell are no longer alien to them. Young guinea pigs are still shy and have to form a closer attachment to their owner. Proceed gradually when you hand-tame your new pet.

The first step: Hold out a carrot or a piece of apple as you talk gently to the guinea pig. You need to be patient. It won't dare approach you right away, but may sniff a little in your direction. Once it takes the treat from your hand, the ice will be broken.

The second step: Now you can scratch its head gently and gradually proceed to the back. When it stops shrinking from your touch, you have gained its trust.

The third step: Since the guinea pig is no longer beside itself with fear, you should take it out of its cage from time to time and set it on your lap. Your relationship will become closer and closer. The amount of time required for these three steps will vary, depending on your guinea pig. It is essential not to lose patience. If your child has been longing for a playmate, you need to explain this to them. Your child can be certain that given time, even the shyest guinea pig will eat from his or her hand.

Note: Always speak to the guinea pig in a low, even voice, and be slow and deliberate in your movements. Otherwise, the animal will be frightened and be very slow to gain confidence.

By rubbing noses or checking the anal area guinea pigs can determine who belongs to the pack.

This is how two guinea pigs that are strangers to each other can sniff each other out and get to know each other without risk of conflict.

Becoming Acquainted with Other Guinea Pigs

This is a sociable species: it is better to keep two guinea pigs than one. Nevertheless, you need to be careful if you plan to introduce another guinea pig as a companion for an established pet.

You also do not want to unnecessarily endanger the pet that you have grown to love. It is entirely possible that the new animal is carrying a disease that has not yet surfaced. It is advisable, therefore, to keep the newcomer in a separate cage for three weeks, until you can be sure that it really is healthy. To help them get acquainted, proceed as follows:

■ At first, put the cages side by side, so that the animals can see and sniff each other. Later on, open the cage doors to let them visit each other while still remaining on home turf.

■ Put both guinea pigs on your lap, pet them, and let them sniff at each other.

■ Once the animals have demonstrated that they can

101

get along, put them in the same cage. Before you do so, you might want to put perfume on your hands and pet them. Then each guinea pig's own scent will be masked for some time, and the animals will smell alike and get along well.

Getting Used to Other Pets

Animal lovers often have a number of other four-legged or beaked pets around the house. It is important to take into account the individual needs of each species, since not every animal speaks a language in which the guinea pig is also fluent (see pages 19 and 20). Sometimes close friendships develop; other times, your labor of love is all in vain.

To get your new housemate acquainted with your existing pet, it is always best to proceed in three stages. However, do not begin the following exercises until the guinea pig has settled in and is familiar with its human family.

Exercises for a Dog and a Guinea Pig

1 Leash the dog and bring it up to the cage. Talk to it quietly, pet it, praise it for friendly behavior; if it barks,

Can Guinea Pigs Be Trained?

It would be fun if you could teach your guinea pig to dance on its hind legs or to jump through a tire. Unfortunately it isn't supple enough to perform tricks like that. In addition, it doesn't have the capacity for doing something on command. Nevertheless, using treats, you can get it to do all kinds of "gymnastics." Food, in general, is a very considerable factor in the life of a guinea pig. It will therefore get up on its hind legs to reach a lettuce leaf, and that makes it look as if it's dancing.

Guinea pigs also react to music. If you play a little music every time you serve food to your pet (use soft sweet tones—loud noises frighten guinea pigs), it will soon learn to come bustling up to the music alone.

Cute as a button and huggable sweet. There is little danger of the guinea pig scratching or biting.

scold it and give the leash a sharp backward tug.

2 Put the guinea pig on your lap. It will be at the dog's eye level, and the dog cannot dominate it. Let the dog sniff, but hold tightly to the leash. Respond to aggressive behavior by scolding and scooting your chair away sharply. Otherwise, praise the dog and pet both animals.

3 Once the dog shows that it is peaceable, let the guinea pig loose in the room. With your hand on the dog's collar, approach the guinea pig. Talk to the dog quietly, pet it, and let it loose if its behavior is friendly. It must not chase the guinea pig—the little creature would be frightened to death.

Exercises for a Cat and a Guinea Pig

1 Let the cat go up to the cage. Pet it, talk to it lovingly, and scold it if it sticks a paw into the cage, but don't scream or fly into a panic. If the cat does not react to scolding, spray a little water on it.

2 Put the guinea pig and the cat on your lap and pet them. Let them smell your hand in turn, so that each has a chance to get used to the new smell.

3 Once the animals demonstrate that they can get along, let the guinea pig loose in the room, but keep the cat on its leash. This exercise is difficult, since a guinea pig that is bustling about appeals strongly to the cat's hunting and play instincts. Do not let the cat off the leash until it shows no inclination to chase the guinea pig.

Training a Guinea Pig

Guinea pigs like to keep busy. If you take advantage of this instinct while your pet is having its outing, you'll be halfway to having it trained.

How to Housebreak a Guinea Pig

Guinea pigs are in the habit of doing their "business" in protected places. For example, they like to deposit pellets in their little house or use a corner of the cage as a toilet area. You can turn this habit to your advantage, by getting your pet used to a certain spot—a litter box—when it is out of its cage as well, either indoors or on a balcony. But quite frankly, not all guinea pigs can be housebroken.

Some guinea pigs get the idea right away. Others need more time. The younger your pet is, the better your chances of success. Don't get discouraged.

What you can do:
■ The very first time you let the guinea pig out of its cage, set up a shallow plastic pan filled with kitty litter or cage bedding, and put a few pellets of feces in it.
■ Keep putting the guinea pig back into the plastic pan. But don't get angry if it hops out the first few times and relieves itself somewhere else in the room.
■ Pick up the little droppings, put them into the plastic pan, and set the guinea pig down on them.
■ Don't yell at your pet, and don't hit it, no matter how gently. That would only upset the animal and make the housebreaking process more difficult.
■ Watch to see whether it has a favorite corner, and set up the toilet pan there.
■ Every time the guinea pig uses its pan, reward it with a treat.
■ Messes on the floor or carpet can be cleaned with a solution of vinegar and water. It will act as a disinfectant, and the smell is not pleasant to the sensitive nose

If you're very patient you can train your guinea pig to be housebroken while out of its cage.

If you plan to put a new cage mate in with a long-time resident animal, it will take time and effort for it to get used to the newcomer.

of the guinea pig. Once feces pellets are dry, they can be easily swept or vacuumed up.

Note: If you give the guinea pig the run of your home, be sure to put a litter box in each room. Block access to hiding places under beds, cupboards, and the like, or cover the floor underneath such pieces of furniture with newspapers.

Problems with Housebreaking

When you let several guinea pigs out of a cage, you soon reach the limits of housebreaking. Keep these points in mind:

■ A male that is constantly courting will always try to spray a female with urine. And if the female is not in heat, she will defend herself with the same "weapon."

■ If several males are out of the cage, they will mark the room by leaving little pellets of feces everywhere.

■ The females are the cleanest. By all means, try the above-described method with them.

Showing Your Guinea Pig

If you would like to show your guinea pig, you should prepare your pet for the event. Animals that come to the judge's table completely unprepared are afraid, run away, and try to hide. They may get into such a state of panic that they will even bite. Don't subject your pet to this panic; aside from everything else, it does not affect the judging favorably.

Exercise 1: Lay a piece of carpeting on a table, or stretch

A treat can be used to "train" guinea pigs to sit up on their hind legs.

TIP

Let the guinea pig run several times a day for about 20 minutes instead of just once a day for an hour. With shorter runs, it will take care of its business afterward in the cage. Don't feed it until after it has had its free run. That way, getting put back into the cage won't seem like a punishment, for it will be able to eat immediately.

some burlap over the tabletop. You need a rough surface; the animal will slip on a smooth one. Set the guinea pig you have selected on the table. If it wants to run away, hold it in place by exerting a slight pressure, pet it, and talk to it kindly. Once it is calmed down, let go of it. Practice until it sees that nothing bad is happening to it and sits still. That may take a few days.

Exercise 2: Next, teach your guinea pig the best way to sit. It should cut a good "figure" and not lie flat on its belly, like a pancake.

Place the animal so that it is squatting on its hind legs and holding its front legs fully extended. In this position it will display its nicely rounded hindquarters and also show the contours of its shoulders, chest, and head quite clearly. Repeat this exercise until the guinea pig understands that adjusting the position of its body and limbs entails no danger of any kind and it successfully maintains its position. Then it will not be afraid when it encounters the hubbub of a show, where it is supposed to cut a "good figure." An animal that sits quietly on the judges' table is more apt to show its good aspects than one that has to be chased down constantly and whose owner is afraid that it will fall.

Note: It should be clear that any defects in the guinea pig's physique cannot be concealed by its position, no matter how becoming.

The animals have to be well prepared for taking part in shows so that they don't get panicky.

Great Ideas for Playing with Your Guinea Pig

Guinea pigs are by no mean boring animals. You just have to recognize their capacities and train them accordingly.

In their wild habitat, guinea pigs are always on the go, running and leaping, playing and hiding. Naturally, they want to satisfy their need for activity when they live in captivity as well.

A Play Corner for Guinea Pigs

Guinea pigs are not the uninteresting animals they so often are thought to be. On the contrary, they have abilities that you can train. As pets they are not challenged by the things that keep them active in the wild. But the capacity remains, and it will lie fallow if the guinea pigs have nothing to satisfy their need for bustle and activity. I have already described how they establish beaten paths in high grass and memorize the entire network, so that they can quickly flee into their dens if danger threatens. An empty floor is not sufficient; on the contrary, the animals will keep pressing close to the wall as they move along, or they will make no use of the opportunities for activity and doze off in boredom.

What you need to do is to create a play corner for your guinea pig. You can create a "landscape" with cardboard boxes and cardboard tubes of various sizes. Change it frequently by moving and rearranging the pieces or by adding new things.

Note: In any event, it is more fun when two play, since "the second" can be another animal—a dwarf rabbit, for example. The animals will encourage each other to leap and hop. A young animal's delight in hopping is especially contagious.

Two animals have been known to join in concerted action, for example, to move an obstacle out of their path. I dare anyone to make a derogatory remark about the intelligence of guinea pigs.

Fun with Colors

Guinea pigs are able to distinguish colors. That was determined by an experiment that you quite easily can duplicate yourself. Set up four plastic bowls of equal size, in the colors red, yellow, green, and blue, at distances of 24 inches (60 cm). Fill only the red bowl with grain feed, leaving the others empty.

Now, from the other end of the room, let a very hungry guinea pig run toward the

bowls. As soon as it ferrets out the filled bowl, carry your pet back to the starting line and let it try again. At some point the animal will understand what is going on. It will make a beeline for the red bowl and head for it unerringly, even if you switch the red bowl to another position.

Sweet Tones

Guinea pigs also react to musical sounds. They are frightened by loud tones, so be sure to try this activity with an instrument that produces sweet sounds, such as a recorder or a small bell. Play a little melody for your pet every time you serve it its food. After a while the guinea pig will come bustling up in response to the melody alone. Alternatively, you can have your pet sit up on its hind legs to get to a treat, while you ring a little bell. After a short time it will start to squeal whenever the bell is rung, without getting any reward in return. Keep in mind, however, that the animal also has to be willing to perform little "stunts" of this kind. Don't force it to do anything. I have yet to hear whether anyone

has trained a guinea pig to dance on its hind legs.

Note: As you see, guinea pigs' pleasure in learning is at its peak when food is involved. But don't let that lead you to be overly generous in handing out treats.

Obstacle Course

If you remember guinea pigs' original way of life, encouraging them to run and leap is quite an obvious thing to do.

Place the cage in the middle of a maze, and use Lego blocks, small building blocks, cardboard boxes, cardboard tubes, and other materials to simulate the network of pathways around it. If you have several guinea pigs, you can organize races. Who can get to the carrot first? Be sure the entire

Children can make use of almost everything in the toy box for their pet's play area.

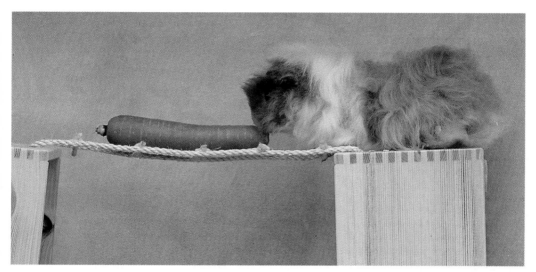

Even a narrow plank is no obstacle to getting at the carrot. But the plank must be stable.

structure has a certain amount of stability; otherwise, the animals will simply knock down the obstacles in their haste to reach their treats. Lay out the paths in such a way that they cannot see over the top and are forced to rely on their nose.

If you distribute edible incentives cleverly, guinea pigs can be motivated to do a whole host of things: for example, they can climb up a ladder, balance across a board, and creep into a cardboard house to climb out through a window on the opposite side.

Note: Rearrange the maze periodically to let the guinea pig have a chance to explore it all afresh otherwise the labyrinth will become boring to your pet.

Sports Inside the Cage

It doesn't take much to get the guinea pigs to do "gymnastics" inside their cage as well.

■ Set the little house on a platform and have the guinea pig reach it by means of a little bridge. Alternatively, place a rock in front of the house so that your pet is forced to climb over it.

■ Separate the feeding area from the sleeping area with a wooden board that has a hole cut in it. Now the guinea pig will have to climb through the hole every time it wants to go from one side to the other.

The Right Way to Solve Behavioral Problems

Crooked feet, long teeth, and coprophagy should no longer be problems now that you have read thus far in the book. But what do you do if the guinea pig, when out of its cage, gnaws on everything or has other "bad habits"?

Eating Carpets and Wallpaper

During its daily run inside your home, your guinea pig constantly undertakes journeys of exploration. In the process it unfortunately gnaws on things better left untouched, for example, carpets, wallpaper, books, newspapers, and paper in general. You are hardly apt to break your pet of this habit. After all, it is following its natural inclination to gnaw, which is quite important in whetting its teeth (see page 59). You must meet its needs as far as possible, so that it will refrain from doing what you oppose. Here are things you can do:

■ Don't leave any kind of paper lying around within the guinea pig's reach.

■ Supervise it during its outing, and clap your hands to chase it away if it goes near the wallpaper.

■ If you catch it gnawing on the wallpaper or the rug, punish it by putting it back in its cage. With the passage of time it may make the connection.

■ Give it dry bread or branches to gnaw. It may be gnawing out of sheer boredom.

■ It is also helpful to move pieces of furniture so that they block your pet's preferred gnawing sites.

Note: There should be no electric cords lying on the floor or accessible in any way when the guinea pig has its run. Gnawing on them could have fatal consequences (see Dangers for Guinea Pigs, page 52).

Gnawing on the Cage Bars

Guinea pigs have been known to gnaw at the bars of their cage even though they have plenty of other things to gnaw on. This behavior may have a number of causes:

■ The guinea pig is very lively and wants to get out of the cage to explore the area.

■ It is alone in its cage and wants to go to its playmate, who is outside the enclosure.

■ The male is in the cage and wants out because he smells a female.

■ Two males are in separate cages side by side. They begin to sharpen their teeth because each one wants to compete with his rival.

■ The guinea pig is hungry and can hardly wait for feeding time.

What you can do:

■ Rub vinegar on the cage bars. Guinea pigs dislike the taste. If that doesn't work with your pet, try another safe substance.

■ Instead of a cage with bars, use a cage top made of plastic (see page 44).

Chewing on the Drinking Bottle

Some guinea pigs tug and tear at the gravity-flow water dispenser and keep chewing at the tube until it's broken. It is unlikely that you will be able to break them of this nasty habit.

You certainly don't want to buy a succession of new gravity-flow water dispensers and must therefore serve animals like that fresh water in a drinking bowl every day.

Avoiding Panic

Some guinea pigs get into a state of real panic when you open their cage and try to take them out. This reaction results from the fact that these defenseless, little animals can seek refuge only in flight (see page 93). If you appear in front of the cage suddenly and thrust your hand into it, the guinea pig will instinctively feel "danger from above: bird of prey." Since flight is not an option in the confines of the cage, panic breaks out. Therefore, avoid the following:

■ Don't put the cage on the floor; set it on something higher, such as a table that does not wobble. You will not seem like a giant and hence a threat.

■ Don't sneak up on the cage. Start talking to your pet in a soothing voice well before you come up to the side of the cage.

■ Don't throw the cage door open; open it carefully. Slowly put your hand in, putting it under the guinea pig's belly from the front; you can coax it with a treat.

■ Never disturb the animal when it's sleeping or eating, for that will aggravate the animal's timid nature.

Note: If you hand-tame the guinea pig in the way outlined on page 100, it will be used to you and have no need to fear you any longer. Unfortunately, there are some "scaredy cats"

who can never really be tamed. Such pets need extra gentle care.

Eating Feces Pellets

Eating feces pellets is not a behavioral disturbance as you might think, a bit revolted. On the contrary, eating excrement from the appendix, which is what is at issue, is a vitally necessary behavioral pattern. Guinea pigs, as well as dwarf rabbits, form the B complex vitamins in their appendix. By eating this excrement which is lighter in color and softer than the usual feces pellets, they're seeing to it that they manufacture the B vitamins for themselves. Young animals who obviously can't yet produce

An earthenware flowerpot is an excellent hideaway.

appendix excrement, get it from their mothers soon after birth (see page 86).

Nibbling at Newspapers under the Bedding

Most of the time, guinea pigs eat the newspapers under the bedding only when there isn't enough hay or straw for gnawing. Other nontoxic materials—for example, toilet paper, paper towels, or blank sheets of paper—can satisfy the animals' need for chewing. If that doesn't help, you can put kitty litter under the bedding. Normally, it won't be necessary to use newspapers under the bedding, if you clean and wash out the cage often enough.

Chewing Hair

Let's say you have two longhaired guinea pigs, and you realize that one is nibbling at the other's hair and has already chewed sizable holes in its companion's coat. Although it does not impair the animal's health, it looks very unattractive.

The bad habit of picking at each other can have several causes:

■ Often it arises from boredom. It is common to many animals that are kept in cages. The poor laying-battery hens are well known for picking out each other's feathers. Provide cage accessories that offer some variety, allow your pet more frequent outings, and give it plenty of attention.

■ Sometimes the animals have too little to nibble on. Make sure they always have enough hay and extremely hard bread or branches available.

■ Usually this bad habit appears in the winter months, when the animals get less fresh food. Even though there is no proven direct link between this deficiency and the behavior, you should offset this deficiency.

Some longhaired guinea pigs have a behavioral disturbance, and there is nothing that can be done about it.

Note: If your guinea pig simply cannot be weaned from this habit—as is sometimes the case, unfortunately—you have to keep it in a cage by itself or put it together with a shorthaired guinea pig. It will be unable to do any damage to the latter's "hairdo."

Excessive Drinking

If a guinea pig drinks excessively any of a number of reasons may be responsible.

■ It may be sick and may have a fever. You should pay prompt attention to this.

■ The animal hasn't had any green food for a long time. Give it fruit and lettuce or gather fresh plants.

■ The animal is drinking too much because it's bored. If this proves to be the case, you should take the bottle out of the cage and hang it up again only for short periods at specific times.

Loner Behavior

Now and then one comes across guinea pigs that segregate themselves from the others. Usually, these are animals that were taken away from their mother very early on and were raised alone. Because of that they lack sense of identification with the group, thus making it very difficult, or impossible, for them to associate with an animal of their own kind. They certainly do develop a great dependency on their human partner and when out of the cage they follow their owner around. It is best to continue to keep such a guinea pig in a separate cage. Or you can try a dwarf rabbit as a partner. This inter-animal friendship usually works out very well (see pages 19 and 20).

Note: Two males that don't get along can't be called loners. They are behaving as nature programmed them by competing for their place and rank in the pack.

Rank Order After Neutering

Let's say you have three females and, without planning for it, you acquire a male. Because you're not interested in offspring, you have it neutered. After that, the male might turn out to be fearful and shy. The females bite him and he's no longer the boss in the cage. The reason for this might be that it was only

after neutering that he was put in with the females who continue to assert their claims as before. Things can take a different turn very quickly, however, as soon as the male is full grown and surpasses the females in size and weight.

If that doesn't happen, you can also try strengthening his self-confidence. Put the male in a separate cage and give him a young guinea pig as a companion. The older male certainly won't allow the youngster to dominate him.

In addition, take special care of him, i.e., take him out as often as possible, pet him, and feed him by hand.

Keeping Several Females

In general, several female guinea pigs will get along very well with each other. Ranking order also exists among females (see page 92). When ranking order is first being determined, there can be quarrels and nipping. But these are usually quickly settled and never have serious wounds as a consequence.

■ If one of the females has already been in the cage for a long time and a second one is introduced, it is quite possible that more severe biting may result. You should then take action. For example, offer a second sleeping house to the new female. It is usually the house that is often the source

An irresistible guinea pig.

of quarrels. If a female has to squat outside because the other one won't let her in, it can be very frustrating to her. But if each one is in her own house, this source of trouble disappears. It is indispensable, of course, that the animals have a big enough cage at their disposal (see page 44).

■ You'll be playing it safe if you put the animals together on neutral territory. They won't get into each other's hair there, since neither one can claim that turf as her own. After they've gotten used to each other, you can put them back into the old cage. Another possibility is petting

both guinea pigs after perfuming your hands and thereby suppressing their own odor for a while (see page 102).

■ There are problems only when one of the females has been kept alone for a long time. They have great difficulty reintegrating into a herd (see "Loner Behavior," page 114). Reintegration works best if the guinea pigs are still very young.

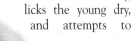

Jealousies

Sometimes a female that had stillborn offspring plays "auntie" alongside another mother-to-be. "Auntie" assists at delivery, licks the young dry, and attempts to

There are occasional loners among guinea pigs too.

"adopt" them. But since she usually has no milk, the children prefer to stick to their real mother. "Smoldering" jealousy can be prevented by petting both females over and over and feeding them separately.

It may be necessary to separate mother and daughter if one of them has offspring. This depends on how well they get along and the size of the cage. If mother and daughter have already had little disagreements, or if the mother-to-be isn't able to withdraw to a quiet corner of the cage, then the pregnant female should be kept alone.

Note: If the mother has just given birth and the older daughter tries to drink from her again, it is better to separate both of them, so that the mother isn't additionally weakened.

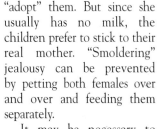

One of Two Guinea Pigs Dies

Usually, the guinea pig left behind visibly grieves, sits in only one corner of the cage, and stops eating. It is far from a sign of contentment if the animal doesn't refuse food. In every case it is best to give it a partner again.

It will without doubt accept a 6- to 10-week-old young guinea pig. Be careful when getting them used to each other and let the two establish contact in the way described on page 101.

Note: It would be presumptuous to try to take the place of the lost partner yourself, even if you spend all day looking after the animal.

Capturing Runaway Guinea Pigs

Don't try running after the guinea pig. It's more nimble and agile than you think.

Instead, put the cage, filled with plenty of straw, in a central spot. The guinea pig may march right into it on its own. If you rustle a paper bag or put a treat into the cage, the process will take less time.

Recapture is easiest if you have several animals. The runaway animal will definitely try to join up with the other guinea pigs again. A male, especially, will try to get back to his female.

Note: You'll succeed in capturing the animal with a net only if you catch it on the first try. If you've struck out, the animal will immediately hide and for a while nothing will get it to venture out.

Transfer to a New Cage

Transferring an individual guinea pig or even a group of animals that are used to each other, usually takes place without a hitch. Stress arises only if a single guinea pig is put in with a new group in which the newcomer has to assert itself, or if several guinea pigs have to share a cage that's much too cramped. Transferring for travel or once a week when cleaning the cage presents no problem.

Transferring guinea pigs from one cage to another usually takes place without a hitch.

My Guinea Pig

Name

Born on

Breeder   Date Bought:

Sex

Breed

Color   Weight on (date):

Distinguishing Characteristics

Favorite Foods

What's Typical of My Guinea Pig

Veterinarian's Name and Address:

Abyssinian, 33, 36
  satin, 33
Age considerations, 28
Agouti, 33–34
Allergies, human, 70
Alpaca, 41
Altering, 17–18
American, 33
  crested, 37, 39
  satin, 33
American Cavy Breeders
    Association, 33
American Rabbit Breeders
    Association, 32
Anal check, 30–31
Anatomical
    characteristics,
    90–91

Bathing, 57–58
Bedding material,
    50–51
Behavior, 31
  loner, 114–115
  problems, 90–97,
    112–117
Beige, 34
Birds, interactions with,
    20
Birth, 83–84
Black color, 34
Bleeding, 74
Boars, 78, 80
Body, 31–32
  language, 96–97
Bone structure, 90

Breathing, 74
Breed:
  origins, 8–13
  special characteristics,
    32
  standard, 32
  unofficial, 41
Breeding, 78–87
  frequency, 85–86
Brindle, 34
Buff, 34
Burns, 52

Cage, 44–46, 48–50
  positioning, 51–52
Capybara, 13
Castration, 17–18
Cats, interactions with, 19,
    53, 103
Cavia aperea, 11, 16
Cavies, wild, 17
Chattering, 94
Chewing, 112
Chirping, 94
Chocolate, 34
Cinnamon agouti, 34
Claws, 29, 91
  growth, 59–60
  sharpening stone, 47
Clucking, 94
Coat, 28, 31–32
  bare patches, 74
  care, 56–57
Colors, 33–34, 108–109
Combing, 58
Commercial food, 66
Conjunctivitis, 75

Constipation, 73–74
Contract, sales, 25
Cooing, 94
Coronet, 41
Coughing, 74
Courtship, 82
Cream, 34

Death, 116–117
Diarrhea, 31, 73–74
Diet, 11
Dogs, interaction with, 19, 102– 103

No amount of twisting and turning is too much to get at the tempting apple.

Domestication, 11
Drinking, excessive, 114
Drooling, 74
Dutch, 35–36
Dwarf rabbits, interactions with, 19

Ears, 31–32
  check, 31
  cleaning, 60
Electrical shock, 52
English crested, 37–38
Equipment, 44–55
Euthanasia, 77
Exercise, 52–53
Eyes, 31–32
  cleaning, 60

Falls, 52–53
Feces, eating, 113–114
Feeding, 54, 66–68
  plan, 69
Feet, 29, 31, 90–91
Food dish, 47–48
Fruit, 64, 66
Fungal diseases, 70

Galea musteloides, 9
Gender considerations, 16–19
Gestation, 11
Gnawing, 112
Golden, 34
  agouti, 34
Gray agouti, 34

Grooming, 56–62
Growling, 94
Grunting, 94

Hair chewing, 114
Hamsters, interactions
    with, 20
Hay, 64
Hayrack, 46–47
Hazards, 52
Head, 32
Health:
    characteristics, 30–31
    problems, 70–75
Hearing, 95
Heat stroke, 52–53, 75
Himalayan, 36
House plants, 52
Housebreaking, 104–106
Housing, 44–55
Hydrochoerus, 10

Illness, 76–77
    symptoms, 72–73
Inbreeding, 80–81

Japanese, 35
Jealousies, 116

Kerodon rupestris, 12

Language, 93–94
    body, 96–97

Lava stone, 47
Legal considerations,
    24–25
    liability, 25
    sales contract, 25
Legs, 32
Length, 11
Liability issues, 25
Life expectancy, 11
Lilac, 34
Limping, 74
Listlessness, 74
Long haired guinea pig, 39
Lymphocytic
    choriomeningitis, 72

Malocclusion, 60–61
Mange, 75
    mites, 70
Mara, 13
Marked varieties, 34–36
Mating, 82–83
Merino, 41

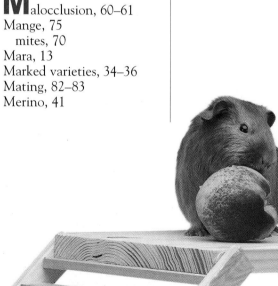

Mice, interactions with, 19
Microcavia australis, 13
Minerals, 66
Multicolored, 34–36
Music, 110

Neutering, 17–18
Newborns, 85
Nidifugous, 86
Nose, 31
    runny, 73
Nutrition, 64–69

Obesity, 68
Obstacle course, 110–111
Ointment, applying, 77
Origins, breed, 8–13
Outdoors, 54–55
Ownership considerations, 14

Pack order, 91–93, 115
Panic, 113
Parasites, 31
    Patagonian cavy, 13
Peruvian, 33, 39
    satin, 33
Pets, other, 19–20
Playing, 108–111
Poisoning, 52, 75
Pregnancy, 63, 83
Pups, development, 86–87
Purchasing, 26–29
Purebreds, 26
    characteristics, 32

Rabbits, interactions with, 19
Rats, interactions with, 19–20
Red, 34
Rex, 37
Rock cavy, 12–13
Rosette, 36
Runaways, 117
Russian, 36

Sales contract, 25
Salmon agouti, 34
Salmonellosis, 70
Satin, 38
Scratching, 74
Self colored, 34
Senses, 95–96
Sexing, 19
Sexual maturity, 85–86
Sheltie, 40
Showing, 106–107
Silkie, 33, 39
    satin, 33
Silver agouti, 34
Single colored, 34
Size, 32
Skin check, 30–31
Sleeping box, 46
Smell, 95–96
Snacks, 66
Snarling, 94
Sneezing, 74
Social interactions:
    children, 20, 98

Climbing a little ladder like this one is no problem for guinea pigs. If they do it several times a day, their need for exercise will be satisfied.

other guinea pigs,
101–102
other pets, 19,
102–103
Sources, 26–29
Sows, 78
Spaying, 17–18
Sputtering, 94
Squealing, 94
Survival traits, 93

Taming, 100
Taste, 96
Tearing, 74
Teddy, 33, 41
  satin, 33
Teeth, 28–30
  chattering, 55
  defects, 75
  growth, 59
Temperature, 53–54
Texel, 37
Tortoiseshell, 35
Touch, 96
Training, 103–107
Travel, 21–23

Tree porcupines, 13
Tschudi cavy, 12
Turtles, interactions with,
20

Vacation care, 20–22
Vegetables, 64
Veterinarian, visit,
76–77
Vision, 95
Vitamins, 66

Washing, 58
Water, 66
  dispenser, 47
Weight, 11, 32
Whimpering, 94
White, 34
  crested, 33
Whorled, 36

Zoological classification,
11–12
Zoonoses, 70

Useful Addresses

American Cavy Breeders
   Association
22859 Fall Leaf Road
Linwood, KA 66052

(Note: The American Cavy Breeders Association is a "specialty club" of the American Rabbit Breeders Association.)

American Rabbit Breeders
   Association
P.O. Box 426
Bloomington, IL 61701

The American Cavy Breeders Association publishes the American Cavy Breeders Association Guide Book and the ACBA Journal, which is published quarterly.

Other Barron's Books

Behrend, Katrin, Guinea Pigs, A Complete Pet Owner's Manual, Barron's Educational Series, Inc., Hauppauge, NY, 1991.

Piers, Helen, Taking Care of Your Guinea Pigs: A Young Pet Owner's Guide, Barron's Educational Series, Inc., Hauppauge, NY, 1993. (For ages 8 and up.)

Petty, Kate, First Pets: Guinea Pigs, Barron's Educational Series, Inc., Hauppauge, NY, 1995. (For ages 4 to 8.)

There is no food rivalry among sociable guinea pigs. It's share and share alike for all.

About the Author

Katrin Behrend, a journalist and an editor of books about animals, lives in Munich and Italy. Guinea pigs are one of her areas of specialization in the field of pet care.

About the Artist

Renate Holzner works as a freelance illustrator. Her broad repertory extends from line drawings and photo-realistic illustration to computer graphics.

About the Photographer

The photos in this book are by Karin Skogstad with the exception of:

Angermayer: pages 8, 10; Angermayer, Ziesler: pages 13, 16; Okapia/NAS/T. McHugh: page 9

Karin Skogstad has worked as a freelance journalist and photographer since 1979. Animals and plants are her areas of special interest.

A tower for climbing and hiding. It must be solidly constructed so that the guinea pig won't take a tumble.

Acknowledgments

The author and the publisher of this book thank the American Cavy Breeders Association and the various Germa guinea pig associations for their friendly assistance and for the large amount of useful information derived from articles in the associations' newsletters. Thanks go also to veterinarian Dr. Peter Hollmann, for his sound advice on *Preventive Care and Health Problems*.

The photographer thanks Ms. Gaby Maric and Ms. Birgit Nasra for allowing their gorgeous guinea pigs to "model" for the photographs in this book.

Important Note

Some diseases are communicable to humans (see page 70). If your guinea pig shows any symptoms of disease (see page 72), it is absolutely essential to consult a veterinarian. If you have questions about your own health, see your physician.

Some people are allergic to animal hair. If you think you or another member of your family may be allergic, consult a veterinarian before you acquire a guinea pig.

The Photos on the Book's Cover

Front Cover: Holland angora, red-white (large photo) and English Crested Satin, monochrome cream (small photo).

Back Cover: Satin, monochrome red.

First English language edition published in 1997 by Barron's Educational Series, Inc.

Published originally under the title *Das Meerschweinchen (Mein Heimtier)*

All inquiries should be addressed to:

Barron's Educational Series, Inc.
250 Wireless Boulevard
Hauppauge, New York 11788

Library of Congress Catalog Card No. 97-70384

International Standard Book Number 0-8120-6596-4

Printed in Hong Kong

987654321